TIME *for* TRUTH

ALSO BY NICK BUNICK

In God's Truth

Transitions of the Soul

TIME *for* TRUTH

A NEW BEGINNING

NICK BUNICK

HAY HOUSE, INC.
Carlsbad, California • New York City
London • Sydney • Johannesburg
Vancouver • Hong Kong • New Delhi

Published and distributed in the United States by: Hay House, Inc.: www.hayhouse.com • ***Published and distributed in Australia by:*** Hay House Australia Pty. Ltd.: www.hayhouse.com.au • ***Published and distributed in the United Kingdom by:*** Hay House UK, Ltd.: www.hayhouse.co.uk • ***Published and distributed in the Republic of South Africa by:*** Hay House SA (Pty), Ltd.: www.hayhouse.co.za • ***Distributed in Canada by:*** Raincoast: www.raincoast.com • ***Published in India by:*** Hay House Publishers India: www.hayhouse.co.in

Editorial supervision: Jill Kramer • *Design:* Riann Bender

Library of Congress Cataloging-in-Publication Data

Bunick, Nick.
Time for truth : a new beginning / Nick Bunick. -- 1st ed.
p. cm.
ISBN 978-1-4019-2754-7 (tradepaper : alk. paper) 1. Jesus Christ--New Age movement interpretations. 2. Bunick, Nick. I. Title.
BT304.93.B86 2010
232.9--dc22
2010013680

Tradepaper ISBN: 978-1-4019-2754-7
Digital ISBN: 978-1-4019-2933-6

13 12 11 10 4 3 2 1
1st edition, September 2010

Printed in the United States of America

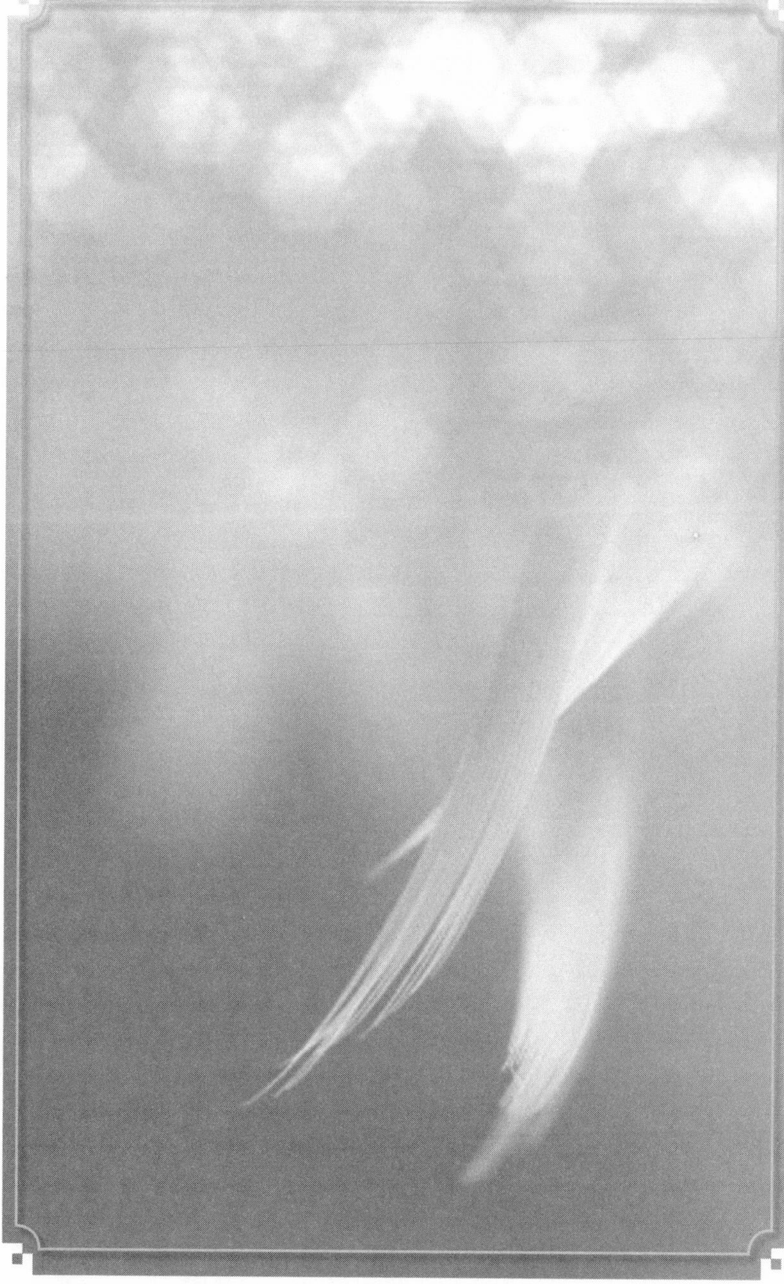

CONTENTS

Introduction

You are about to begin a journey that will change your life forever. But there are no tollgates, no fees to pay, no tickets you have to purchase in order to take this journey. There is, however, a requirement on your part: you must be willing to embark upon it with an open mind and an open heart, for you will be taken places you did not know existed.

If you are a believer in a Divine source, convinced that there is indeed a God, your belief will be enhanced beyond what you would have thought possible, and you will have a greater understanding than ever of how God intervenes in your life. If you are an agnostic, one who acknowledges that you don't know if there is a Divine being, you will no longer be comfortable wearing that mantle. At the end of this journey, that "hat" will no longer fit.

And if you believe yourself to be an atheist, I offer you a challenge: Read this book and discover the truth for yourself. Find some explanation for what you've experienced here other than the fact that you are a child of God. Your life will never be the same, and you will find the answers to the most important questions that humankind has posed throughout history.

In the first two portions of this book, I will share many miracles with you. I define a miracle as the intervention of God in our lives, but I'll only recount those that I myself have witnessed, or those of which I was the beneficiary. I don't believe I would have the commitment, or perhaps even the courage, to share the third part of this book if I hadn't had the experiences I'll share with you in the first two sections of *Time for Truth.*

You may already know that in 1997 I was the subject of the best-selling book *The Messengers.* During the first six months after it was published, I received more than 10,000 letters, and I soon found myself traveling around the country speaking in front of thousands of people, and on television and radio speaking to millions. People around the world started to have the same experiences I had, which are described in the pages of *The Messengers.* They began to receive absolute proof that they also had spirit guides in their lives, and many saw angels standing behind me on the stage as I spoke.

I've never seen an angel, for I am not clairvoyant. I've never heard words from the spiritual world, for I am not clairaudient. But I discovered around 1994 that I had become *claircognizant*—that is, my spirit guides would communicate with me in my mind as if by some means of telepathy. Just like I could use my memory to access the activities I'd performed the day before, my guides would provide me with information, oftentimes extremely profound, which I could retrieve in a similar fashion.

I also discovered that my guides gave me the ability to channel information in writing from the spiritual world. There were times I would find material in my handwriting that I had no recollection of having written. Other times I would receive the message that my guides wanted to share something with me, and I discovered that I was able to sit with a pencil and paper, or in front of a typewriter or computer keyboard, and place my conscious mind aside in a state of quiet; then somehow the channel would open and the words would flow out, which I would capture on paper. Many of these profound messages will be relayed to you throughout these pages.

On this journey we'll be taking together, I'll share true stories that have no explanation other than this: we are eternal and immortal, and there is no such thing as death. I'll provide you with what I believe is irrefutable evidence that we are not humans who by coincidence have a spirit and soul, but rather, we are spirits with a soul who are having a human experience.

I myself discovered that I was the reincarnation of a person who lived 2,000 years ago and walked with the Master Jesus. I rejected this information for more than ten years, even when the proof became overwhelming. But after I spent six months in past-life hypnotic regression and accessed the entire memory of that lifetime centuries ago, I couldn't reject it any longer. Even at that time I didn't share this information with many others, however. Then God, my angels, and my spirit guides brought into my life many witnesses who either were with me when I experienced a Divine intervention or who also began to have these same experiences themselves. Only then did I have the courage to step forward. And what I've just written is only a portion of what you'll read about in the first two parts of this book.

The third section of this work deals with some of the greatest problems we have in the world and their causes. For example, religion has failed humanity. How many millions of people over the last 2,000 years have been tortured and murdered in the name of God? Did those who were responsible not know that the greatest "sin" that can be committed is one *performed* in the name of God?

I'll share with you how the messages of Jesus and Paul 2,000 years ago have been distorted. How messages of love were warped into ones of fear. How messages of compassion were changed into ones of guilt. How messages that were supposed to bring us together as brothers and sisters were altered to polarize people, not the least of which is that God was and is a punishing deity.

You will learn how legitimate teachings were rewritten in order to control the lives of the Catholic Church's followers. You will learn the true reason behind the death of Jesus, and how and why these facts have been manipulated. And why, as stated in the subtitle of this book, it is time for . . . *A New Beginning.*

After *The Messengers* was published, one of the letters I received was from a man named John Lawrence, whom I got to know on a personal basis and who was also a tremendously gifted psychic. A few years ago I got a letter from a person who explained that he was John's caregiver and that his employer had asked him to write to me. He said that John told him I would be going on a spiritual mission that would take me around the world, and I would share messages that would impact the lives of millions of people. He also said that if I knew of John's extraordinary psychic gifts, I would take this information very seriously.

I wrote back and asked him to get more information from John. What event or catalyst would enable me to be in a position to influence the lives of so many others? Two months later, I got a reply—unfortunately, it was to tell me that at the age of 92, John had made a soul transition.

John was the first of five seers from five different parts of the world who didn't know each other but who each gave me the same message: that I would be traveling internationally on a spiritual mission, and that my messages would impact the lives of millions. But I had no idea how this would come to pass. I used to jokingly think that I might be in a stadium someday watching a football game, and in front of 50,000 people be beamed up to a UFO and then returned a year later in the same way. How else might this happen?

Then my spirit guides again intervened in my life, two nights in a row (as I'll explain in Chapter 1), which gave birth to *Time for Truth*. And now I know that this book, this journey that you're going to take with me, will launch my mission, as foretold to me by a number of highly evolved spiritual individuals. And I have made the commitment to accept this responsibility and to embark on this mission. So buckle your seat belt . . . the ride is about to start.

God bless you as you take this journey with me.

— **Nick Bunick**

PART I

My Background, Calling, and Mission

Chapter 1

Angelic Messages

More than 30 years ago I was thrown into a world I didn't know existed. At that time I was a successful businessman managing three companies I owned, residing in a beautiful home on a private lake in Oregon, basically enjoying life and living the American Dream. But I had never forgotten my roots.

I'd grown up in a very poor suburb of Boston. My parents never owned a car or a home or had a savings account, and my college expenses at the University of Florida were paid for by a football scholarship. So my appreciation for the blessings I'd been given was permanently ingrained within me.

Then events occurred that changed my life; and when these experiences were shared with hundreds of thousands of others through the publication of the book *The Messengers,* they changed their lives, too.

The year was 1977, and I'd been reluctantly persuaded to make an appointment with a psychic. I had an image of a person wearing a turban, sitting in front of a crystal ball, but Duane Berry was nothing like that. When I walked into his humble kitchen, I found a young man sitting in a trance with his eyes closed, spiritual music softly playing in the background, and incense burning.

I hadn't told Duane's wife my name when I made the appointment, and since his eyes remained closed until the reading was over, the young man wouldn't have known if I was 15 or 50. Yet he proceeded to tell me everything that was happening in my life.

Duane then said that there would come a time when I'd be speaking in front of thousands of people, and to millions on television and radio. I thought that perhaps he meant I'd run for political office and someday be appointed to the U.S. Cabinet or be a United Nations ambassador. But he said, "No, it has to do with the time you walked with the Master 2,000 years ago."

After a number of other psychics, all independent of one another, told me that I was the reincarnation of a man who had lived two millennia ago and had walked with the Master Jesus, I eventually agreed to allow myself to be hypnotized by a professional in the field of past-life regression (Julia Ingram), and be taken back 2,000 years. I didn't have a belief in reincarnation at that time, had never read the New Testament, and didn't practice a religion. I considered myself to be a no-nonsense businessman, not a New Age person, even though I had developed a newfound respect for psychics. But after six months of regularly being past-life-regressed, I did indeed find that I had accessed the entire memory and life of the Apostle Paul.

My memories began as a child running through the fields on Paul's father's estate in Tarsus, in the region of Cilicia, which today is known to be in Turkey. After completing his education, Paul traveled to the Holy Land and made his new home in Jerusalem. At the age of 21, he met Jesus, who was 23, and developed an intense and close personal relationship with him. Paul's friend was actually known as Jeshua, as Jesus was the name the church gave him 350 years later (Jesus is the Greek translation of "Jeshua"). I will refer to him as Jeshua from this point on, for I'm more comfortable calling him by his real name.

Under hypnosis, I was able to provide the details of many events in the lives of both Paul and Jeshua that had never been known before. Also, I was to discover several years later that there were many conflicts between what I'd experienced during my hypnotic state and what is written in the New Testament, but I didn't know why at that time. These discrepancies would later lead me on a quest for the truth.

The Angels Intervene

All of the regression sessions were captured on tape and then transcribed into a manuscript that Julia, the hypnotist, and I titled *He Walked with the Master*, not knowing that it would later become the second half of the best-selling book *The Messengers*. There were four major New York companies that wanted to publish the manuscript, but I chose not to allow this. I didn't have the courage to go forward. I concluded that to do so would destroy my professional career and my personal life and adversely affect my family, since I felt that people wouldn't believe that I was the reincarnation of such a prominent historical figure. They would think I either fabricated the whole story or was insane. As far as I was concerned, having made the decision not to publish the book, it was a closed matter. I thought I'd placed this story into a compartment and sealed the door, which would remain closed forever.

I soon discovered that an idea of God's cannot be defeated. On January 14, 1995, I had the first of many spiritual experiences that changed my life forever. I was told by Spirit that all of us have the gift of free will, but that "they" would bring so many witnesses into my life that I might indeed change my mind and gain the confidence to have the manuscript published. (I honestly don't know if the messages I receive are coming from one spiritual entity or a group of them collectively.) They told me that many events would occur involving the number 444, which would help me make the decision to allow the story to be shared with the world. They said that 444 referred to the power of God's love and that our spirit guides ("angels," if you prefer) are with us, caring for us.

That night I received a phone call from a man I'd only met once at a conference in Seattle. He was a Canadian who was in Geneva, Switzerland, on business. He told me that he'd been fast asleep in bed at his hotel when something suddenly woke him up. After looking at the clock and seeing that it was 4:44 A.M., he felt compelled to call me but didn't know why.

Due to the time difference between Switzerland and my location (the West Coast of the U.S.), his 4:44 A.M. on Sunday was Saturday evening for me. I realized later that not only had the spirit guides awakened him at 4:44, but they'd also made sure that he looked at the clock. And then they had him call *me,* almost a total stranger, to tell me he had been awakened at 4:44 in the morning. Had he called someone else, such as his mother in Calgary or his wife in Vancouver, his phone call wouldn't have had any relevance.

Two days later I arrived at my office on Monday morning at the usual hour and found a friend, Rick Eckert, standing in the reception area. He told me he had woken up in the middle of the night, which he said never happens to him, and had felt compelled to get a pencil and paper and write down many things that he didn't understand, but which he knew he was meant to give to me.

He handed me five sheets of paper, and on the top of the first one was the time 4:44 A.M. And many other things he had written down echoed the information that had been given to me by my spirit guides two days earlier, on that Saturday afternoon.

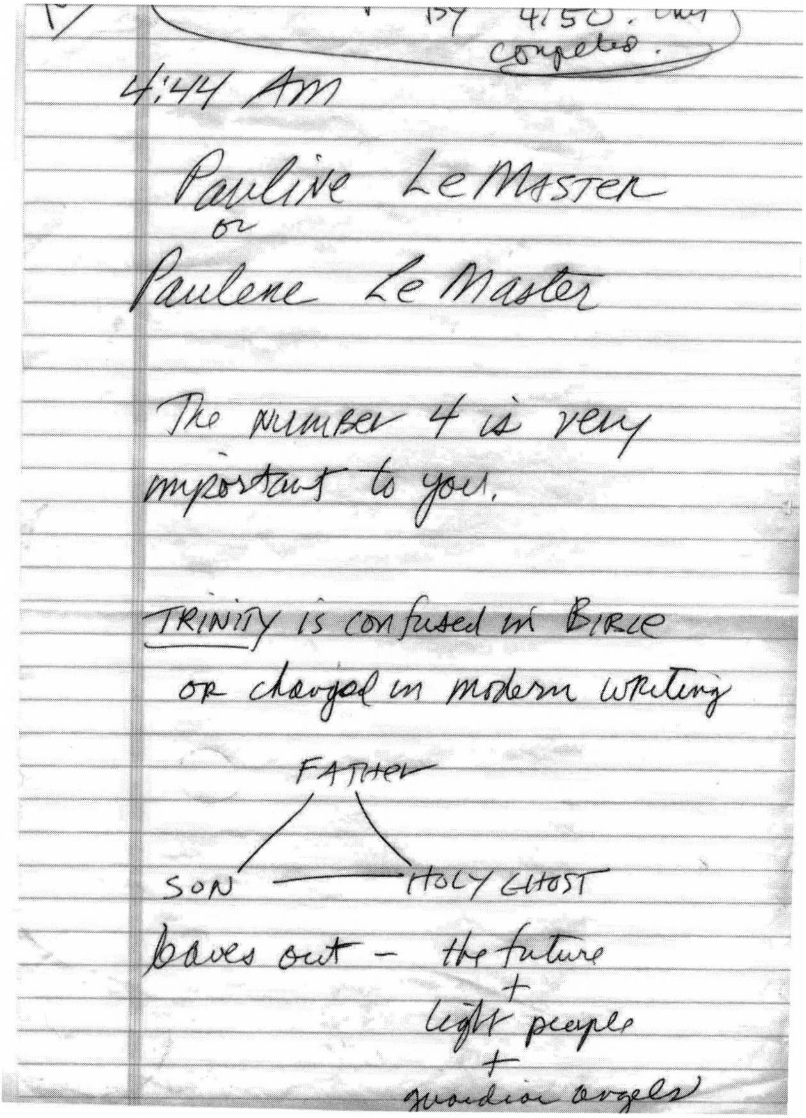

By 4:50. ... completed.

4:44 AM

Pauline LeMaster
or
Paulene LeMaster

The number 4 is very important to you.

TRINITY is confused in Bible or changed in modern writing

FATHER

SON — HOLY GHOST

leaves out — the future
+
light people
+
guardian angels

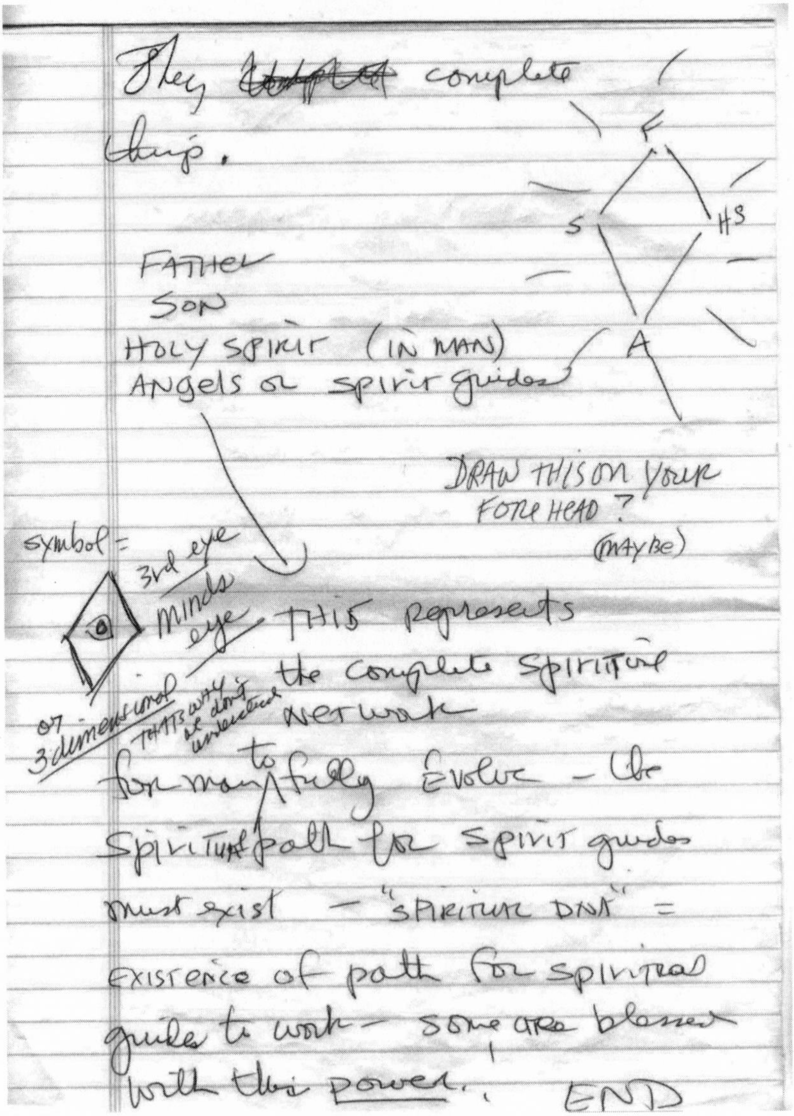

They complete
thing.

F
S
HS
A

FATHER
SON
HOLY SPIRIT (IN MAN)
ANGELS or spirit guides

DRAW THIS ON YOUR FOREHEAD ?
(MAYBE)

symbol = 3rd eye
minds eye
THIS represents
the complete spiritual
network
or
3 dimensional
THAT'S WHY we don't understand
for man to fully Evolve – the
Spiritual path for spirit guides
must exist – "SPIRITUAL DNA" =
existence of path for spiritual
guide to work – some are blessed
with this power. END

Many people around me began to have 444 experiences related to the time of day, many of them extraordinary. (Eventually this would expand to include other 444 incidents unrelated to the clock, as described in the next chapter.) My wife and I also experienced this phenomenon on a number of occasions, which included the following:

- Our infant child routinely woke up at night crying, and when we'd look at the clock, it would be 4:44 A.M.
- The phone once rang at 4:44 A.M., with nobody on the line. When I punched in the code to find out who had called, the operator's voice said that the last call had been at 9:15 P.M.
- The next night I took the phone off the hook when we went to bed, and at 4:44 A.M., the receiver began making the noise it does when it's first taken off the hook.

My wife, who is a Catholic, was as amazed by these events as I was.

I began to keep a journal of all these occurrences. One morning I was woken up at 4:44, and my spirit guides informed me telepathically that a new book of my experiences would be written in Seattle. I didn't know anybody in that city who was a writer, so I then went back to sleep. But when I woke again two and a half hours later, the information they provided me through claircognizance was still very much on my mind. They had told me, absolutely, that a new book would be written.

A Bestseller Is Born

When I arrived at my office, where my staff and I managed my company's real-estate-development activities, I found a phone message waiting for me from a man in Seattle whose name was Gary Hardin. I called him back, and Gary reminded me that he'd met me the previous summer when the company he then worked for had wanted to publish my manuscript, *He Walked with the Master.* He said that he didn't know why he was now calling me.

I related the events that were transpiring in my life and told him about the journal I was keeping. Gary asked if he could have a copy of it, which I did send to him. After reading it, he called again, this time to ask me if he could write a manuscript—the first half of which would consist of all my spiritual/angelic experiences from the journal, and the second half comprising the transcriptions of the hypnotic sessions that were in *He Walked with the Master.* I asked Gary how long it would take to write the manuscript, and he said probably four months.

He sent me chapters as they were being written, and I told him he was doing a fantastic job. Gary would laugh and say, "Nick, something else is writing this," and the book was indeed finished . . . in just four weeks. I decided to call it *The Messengers,* with Gary Hardin and Julia Ingram, who did the regressions, being the co-authors.

After we self-published it in late 1996, the book became an instant bestseller and was then acquired by a major New York publishing company. Of the more than 10,000 letters we received in the first six months, over half of the writers described having had 444 experiences. They even created an international Website called the "444 Forum" where people shared these experiences.

I soon found myself traveling around the U.S. giving presentations in front of large audiences, as well as appearing on television and radio (just as the psychic had predicted in 1977). From my office, I was doing about six or seven talk-radio shows a week, and that was when I found out that there were many conflicts between my story as depicted in *The Messengers* and what had been written in the New Testament.

The discrepancies were so great and so profound that I was determined to find out why. Where did the truth lie? Was it in the Bible or in my memories as Paul? It took me many years of research to discover the truth: I learned that when the Catholic Church was founded in the 4th century, the leaders had made a deliberate decision to alter the teachings of Jeshua and Paul. They did so for many reasons, the foremost being their intention to control the lives of the people through fear rather than love.

I also discovered that the Christianity we know of today did not begin with the birth of Jeshua, or when Paul began forming churches throughout the Roman Empire. It actually began with one event that occurred in A.D. 312, which I will describe in detail in Chapter 17.

Time to Wake Up

I do now believe with all my heart and soul that it is *Time for Truth.* There are many things I'm going to share with you that I know will have a positive impact on your life, as well as the world—for, as I mentioned, a number of different seers in different parts of the globe told me of the mission I would have before me, which would begin with this book.

There is one last bit of information that I want to share with you before we move forward. One night recently I was lying in bed, and I was awakened at 4:44 A.M. I looked at the clock, smiled, and went back to sleep. The following night the lamp on the table next to my bed turned on while I was asleep. As I sat up, puzzled, intending to turn it off, I looked at the clock . . . and it was 4:44 A.M. I got up and kneeled by my bedside and prayed for guidance. Spirit told me to contact Hay House, the company that has now published the work you have in your hand, and tell them that I had a book inside me that I had to write and that they had to publish; and that is how you and I have been brought together today.

So now it is *Time for Truth.* . . . In the next chapter, we shall explore the incredible 444 phenomenon in more depth.

Chapter 2

444 Experiences

It was two o'clock in the afternoon on January 14, 1995, when the angels told me that the number 444 would play a very important part in my life. In reality, it had already *been* part of my life, but I hadn't realized it. For three years in high school and for the duration of college, my football number was 44. Likewise, at the time of that angelic experience, the code for the phone message-retrieval system in both my home and office was 444, as was the security-system password at my house. Yet I wasn't even consciously aware of any of these things.

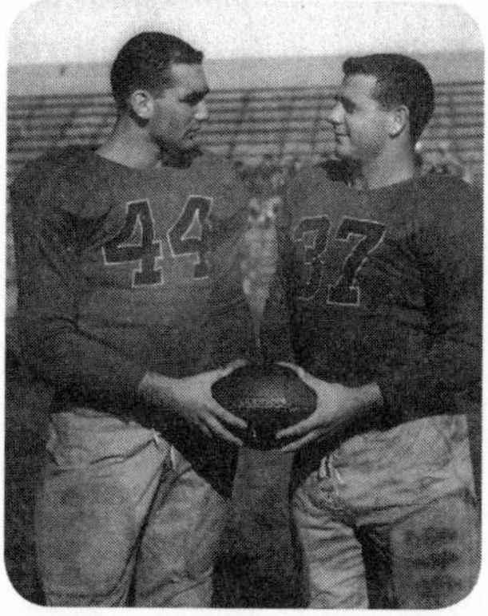

Me [left] wearing my high-school football jersey.

Me wearing my college jersey.

As I mentioned in the last chapter, following the publication of *The Messengers*, thousands of people all over the world began to have 444 experiences. To this day I still average about five letters a week from readers, including people who are just finding the book 13-plus years later. I can assure you with confidence that the same will happen again: thousands who are reading *this* book will begin to have 444 experiences, and I'll be hearing about it for years to come.

And now that *you* have knowledge of the relationship between you and your angels and guides, that door—that line of communication—will be open. In fact, I'll provide you with my new Website at the end of this book, which will enable you to share your 444 experiences with other readers.

The 444 phenomenon represents two things:

- **First**, it is an expression of the "power of God's love." It is an indication of God's relationship with you, such as a loved one getting flowers, or a special greeting card from someone.
- **Second**, it is one of the ways in which your spirit guides let you know that they are in your life. Many people have had unexplained 444 experiences for years without ever realizing it.

Many people have also informed me that they've had 111 experiences, which I don't have, but which I assume have a spiritual significance as well.

Some of the 444 experiences have been extraordinary. I want to share one of the most unusual ones I had, which took place in London in 1995.

I was staying at a hotel in which each guest had two rooms: a modest-sized bedroom and a small parlor with a sofa, a TV, and an armoire. Sitting atop the armoire, which was about seven feet tall, was a very large, ornate clock encased in glass. It was round on top, and the glass came all the way down to the wood frame at its base.

One night as I lay in bed, I prayed that the angels would give me a sign that they were with me and still supporting my efforts. That was my last thought before I fell asleep. The next morning I went into the parlor to turn on the TV to watch the news while I was getting dressed, and I was startled to see the three hands of the clock—the hour, the minute, and the second—all frozen on the number 4. Normally if the hour and minute hands had been together near the 4, it would be 4:20, and the hour hand would actually be slightly *past* the 4. But in this case, all three hands were *precisely* on it, as if someone had removed the glass enclosure and manually forced them to hover over that number.

It was such a dramatic sight that I went to my knees and prayed silently in acknowledgment for several minutes. I felt a great sense of comfort, knowing I was loved and that my guides were with me.

Personal 444 Stories

Here are a couple more personal experiences I've had involving the number sequence 444:

— I was having phone conversations regarding humanitarian projects with a woman from upstate New York who was the trustee of an organization that provided funding for various nonprofit companies. She told me of a friend of hers, a lady in her 30s, who had been diagnosed with terminal cancer. She asked me if I would pray for her, and I said yes. I also told the woman I'd send her *The Messengers,* which hadn't yet been published, and asked her to have her friend read it.

Several days later the woman called me again, crying. She told me that prior to receiving the manuscript, she had woken up three nights in a row at exactly 4:44. She'd told her friends she couldn't account for this strange phenomenon of waking up at that unusual hour on three consecutive nights. When she received my manuscript and read the second chapter, regarding my 444 experiences, she wept with joy.

She then shared my material with her friend, and I talked to both of them on the phone several times. It wasn't too long afterward that her friend was told by the doctors that she no longer had cancer. She had been healed by her greatly enhanced faith and the power of God's love.

— When the book was released, I had a friend of mine, Doug Fish, who owned his own advertising agency, do some local marketing. When he logged my account into his company books, he discovered that I was his 444th client. Shortly thereafter, he was awakened very early in the morning to use the bathroom and saw that the clock showed it was 4:44. The next morning when he turned on his computer, the numbers 444 in a large digital format were flashing on his screen.

— Another dear friend of mine is also my attorney, Mark Wagner. He was an agnostic, and very skeptical of the experiences I shared with him. One day he called to tell me he was in the hospital. He had been cutting down a huge maple tree in his yard, and it had fallen on him, landing across his back.

He asked, "What time do you think I was admitted to the hospital?"

I told him I didn't know.

He said, "Nick, it was at 4:44. What room do you think they put me in?"

I asked if it was room 44.

"No," he replied, "it was room 444." He said the doctors told him it was a miracle that he hadn't been killed. He is no longer an agnostic.

— I had lunch with another skeptical friend, Jim Stewart, and told him about the 444 experiences. He laughed, stating that these must have all been coincidences.

The next day he and his family went to Florida on a vacation. A week later he called me, very excited, and told me I must come over to his house right away. He and his family had just returned that day from Disney World, and when they entered their home, they found that the large digital clock in their kitchen was pulsating with the numbers 4:44.

The 444 Letters

Let me share excerpts from a few of the letters we have received from people all over the world:

Kathy, May 24, 1997

The afternoon after I finished your book, I was driving to work and said, "If I have any angels with me, please communicate in some way so that I know for sure." When I arrived, there was a new person sitting at my desk, so I took my work into the lunchroom. I was alone when all of a sudden the microwave beeped twice. No one was using it. I looked up and the time was 4:44. I had a huge grin on my face and was staring at the microwave when a co-worker came in to ask me a question. She looked at the microwave and then at me—I know she thinks I lost it, but I was so happy.

Pamela, September 16, 1997

I had been reading The Messengers one night and then fell asleep. I woke up and thought I had better go to the bathroom. When I returned, I decided to look at the digital clock to see what time it was. To my amazement, the clock said 4:44—not 4:43, not 4:45. A sense of joy and excitement came over me. I couldn't wait to share this with my roommate, who also began to have 444 experiences after she read the whole book! It's just amazing!

Audra, August 12, 1997

Yes, I know I wrote you earlier, but something else happened today, another 444 incident. I have always had a strange connection with my cousin and would often have the urge to call her. She'd generally reply that she'd been thinking about me—so I've gotten to the point where I can just say, "What is it?" instead of hello. I had that urge tonight and told her about your book—I just finished reading about the 444s. She said,

"Would you laugh if I told you that for the last four nights I have been waking up at 4:44 A.M.?! It also just so happens I have been reading the same book for the last four days!"

Emanuel, April 10, 1998

First of all, I would like to say that I enjoyed your book tremendously. I have just finished reading it for the second time. It is very uplifting and heartwarming.

A friend of mine bought the book for me in July of '97. I have read quite a few angel books since my 16-year-old son was shot and killed on September 15, 1996.

I am quite sure I had a 444 experience right after I read your book the first time. I had just finished it and gone to the grocery store. As I pulled out of the store's parking lot, a van pulled out ahead of me. I looked at the license plate and it read "AMA-444." The name of my late son is Anthony Mario Arruda, his initials being AMA. So, when I saw the license plate, I was shocked, seeing as how I had just finished reading your book that morning. I know in my heart it was no coincidence, because God is no coincidence. God bless you and your wonderful story.

There are so many different ways in which your angels and guides may wish to let you know that they're in your life. It could be by waking you up at 4:44, clocks or watches stopping at that time, 444 flashing on your computer screen, or fire and security alarms going off at 4:44.

Several people wrote to say they were given room 444 when they checked into a hotel. I've also gotten reports of a light coming on at 4:44, a phone ringing at that time with nobody on the line, or a purchase yielding $4.44 in change.

Just remember, this is your spirit guides' way of letting you know they are in your life, and demonstrates the power of God's love for you.

But there are other ways in which Spirit can communicate with you. In the next chapter, I'll discuss the incredible and profound experience of receiving written messages from one's guides.

Chapter 3

CHANNELED WRITINGS

The very first time I became aware of Spirit writing messages through me was many years ago. I found some words in my handwriting on a piece of paper on my office desk. I had no recollection of having written them, and it took me several years to realize they came from a higher source. But I cherished those words and placed the paper under the glass-top cover of my desk, where it sat for many years. It simply read: *"Enjoy life every moment. Let others enjoy life through you."* So simple, yet so profound.

Several years later I decided to make a conscious effort to receive information from Spirit by writing down words on paper as they were provided to me. I vividly remember that night many years ago, sitting by a small writing table in my bedroom, trying to focus my mind to accept my guides' words. I was positive that nothing had happened. I don't know how long I sat in that chair before I finally gave up and went to bed.

The next morning when I woke up, I walked over to the table to put the paper and pencil away. I was startled to find words on the paper in my handwriting. There were three separate sets of sentences:

1. *"The rain cannot distinguish need. It falls both on the ocean as well as in the valley."*
2. *"God's love is like sunshine, but there are some that prefer to remain in the shade."*
3. *"Rejoice with the birth of every blade of grass, for it is a gift from God."*

I have thought of those words many times over the years. I've tried to decipher their meaning, often coming up with different conclusions. At one time I decided that the first set of sentences meant that there are times we receive things that may or may not be beneficial to us, and we have to be discriminating in what we accept. Other times the words meant something else to me. Perhaps they will also signify something to you that is personal, according to your interpretation and circumstances.

Over the years I have received many dozens of messages from my spirit guides in this way. Sometimes I'm even able to get them deliberately while awake. I place my mind in a state of stillness, setting my conscious self aside. I am aware of what is transpiring and write down the words as they are given to me, as if through some form of telepathy.

Other times I've received words while in a state of meditation or a trance, perhaps, for I have no recollection of having written them. Yet I would find them handwritten on sheets of paper, sometimes even in drawers or files, possibly months after I wrote them.

The following is an example of a poem with no date on it that I found in a folder in a filing cabinet. Again, I did not create these words—Spirit did. The theme of the poem is what may be going though the soul mind of a baby during birth—that is, the feelings and thoughts of a soul being incarnated into his new life.

From Spirit to Birth

The moment had come to begin
As the infant made his way.
My spirit entered within the babe.
It was to be my birth day.

Where did I dwell before this moment?
What mystical garden or plane?
Why did I choose to be born again?
What did I have to gain?

There is so much I leave behind,
Understanding and love and sharing.
But now to enter a strange new world,
Was my choice made of courage and daring?

The cycle of life must go on.
It is not a matter of choice.
I know that the next sound that I will hear
Of the stranger is my new mother's voice.

It is sad to leave behind
The comfort that was part of me.
To enter the new world of wonders,
Was I to be a he or a she?

I say good-bye to my guides.
You were so wise and so kind.
I know we shall meet again,
For coming to Earth does not break our bind.

Slowly I depart as I enter.
Please, world, help me find my way.
Although I come unable to speak,
There is so much I want to say.

I bring with me thousands of years of wisdom,
Anguish and fear and joy.
The air is so cold and the slap so hard,
And the man says, "You have a boy."

I do not remember the moment
In which my mind became a blank.
But now I must learn all over
To reject, accept, and thank.

It would be so much easier
If we knew what we knew in between.

But it is the way of life
That what we saw does not remain to be seen.

So I shall accept what I must,
And will do my best,
As I continue my journey,
For I know only perfection will end this quest.

You Are a Channel

If you wish to try to channel written messages yourself, it will require great patience on your part, as well as perseverance.

Sit down in a comfortable chair with paper in front of you and a pen or pencil in your hand. Close your eyes and ask for Divine guidance. Tell your spirit guides that you are offering yourself as a channel, and ask them to share a message with you. Then write what comes to your mind.

It may take a few times before you get a result, or a hundred . . . or you may never get a message, because for some reason you may not be a channel for the written word. It's not a case of good or bad, or a matter of your guides loving you or not. That has absolutely nothing to do with it, just as I have no control over my inability to carry a tune or break a golf score of 120 no matter how hard I try; I'm just not programmed in those two areas. On the other hand, it may come to you without any effort.

I once had dinner with a woman whose name is well known in Washington, D.C., because she has been a speechwriter for several presidential candidates, as well as a former vice president. She told me that one day when she was working on a speech, all of a sudden incredible spiritual messages were being typed on her computer without her consent or effort. This had continued to happen every so often for over a month when I met her, and she was startled and frightened by it and asked me to explain what was going on.

This unexpected channeling was also how a journalist named Ruth Montgomery became a famous author. One day while she was typing, her guide, whom she called Lily, began to send her messages. These typed messages from Lily eventually led Ruth to pen bestseller after bestseller. So don't have any expectations or feel disappointment, and let Spirit do as it chooses.

If you aren't able to develop a channel for the written word at all, then be very sensitive to information your guides may be transmitting to you while you're in meditation. If you feel that you're receiving messages, through whatever means, it is absolutely imperative that you discard any that would cause injury—mentally, emotionally, or physically—to you or another. These are not real. Remember, happy thoughts produce happiness as an onion seed produces an onion. Your loving guides would never give you a negative message.

You may also receive messages from your guides while you're asleep. For example, for three nights in a row several years ago, I remember being aware as I awoke that the last scene in my mind was one of a young man. He appeared to be in his early 30s, beardless but with long hair, and he was dressed only from the waist down in a white half toga. He was lecturing to me in a very gentle and loving way.

Although images such as these are compelling, I do believe that channeling the written word from Spirit would produce the most convincing result for you.

Your Soul Mind

One day Spirit had me type the following message—it apparently came from my "higher self," meaning my soul mind rather than my conscious mind:

> *"Nick, you search for truth. Man knows that inside lies all the understanding of the universe, but only he can draw upon that wealth which lies within. What he seeks he shall find. He who does not seek shall never enjoy the riches that are to be known."*

"Who is talking?"

"It is I, yourself. The inner soul, the mind within the shell."

"Are you one of my guides?"

"The self is the being, one and the same. Love and truth is oneness. Those who love you, guide you. You are one."

I'm assuming that what is meant in the last few lines is that my higher self is also a guide for me. Of course, the same would be true for *you.* We all have a soul mind as well as a conscious one. Your soul mind has been with you from the moment you were brought into the world as one of God's children, part of God's own spirit.

Over and over again, preachers and religious teachers speak as if the soul and the spirit are one and the same, which they are not. Perhaps this is a good time to explain the difference between the two:

— The **spirit** is that part of God that is within you, which gives you your immortality. It is what is referred to as the Holy Spirit, for it is of God. The fact that you are alive and reading this book is because part of God's spirit is inside of you, and therefore you have life. The Holy Spirit, which is with you for eternity, is truly within you.

— Your **soul** is the personality of your spirit . . . its value system, intellect, and ambitions; and yes, your soul mind has the memories of every lifetime you've ever lived. It is constantly changing with every experience you have, as you climb farther up the stairs of the pyramid (a concept I'll explain later in the book) to become at one with God and Christ Consciousness.

A Universal Message

This chapter, as you can see, contains a mixture of spiritual messages. As I've shared with you previously, *I* am not the author. Sometimes I envision Spirit sitting at a conference table in front of a transmitter that is somehow connected to my conscious mind, dictating words to me so I may relay them to you.

I feel that the following message is universal, applying to all of God's children. I've reread it countless times over the years, and I hope you will also embrace its meaning, as it applies to you, too. . . .

> *There are many things you devote your attention to in life that are meaningless, that do not warrant the energies that you expend—the worry, the time, the loss of happiness. You must control your energies and center them on things you know will bring you happiness and peace of mind. You are mind, and in being mind, you should not feed yourself negative thoughts (harmful things) any more than you would feed your body harmful things.*
>
> *Control what goes into your mind. Happy thoughts produce happiness. Sad thoughts produce sadness. An onion seed produces an onion. Love is the greatest elixir of all: It cleans your soul; erases negative feelings; and makes you tolerant, patient, caring, interesting, and enthusiastic. It can only bring you good results and overrides any other thoughts and emotions that can be harmful.*
>
> *Learn to live your life flowing with the tide. Accept, and try not to make negative things become unnecessary realities. You have been provided a wonderful capacity for happiness through your intellect and your physical being and your sense of awareness. Be love and gentleness . . . and all around you, you shall create the same. You know you control your own reality; therefore, direct it toward that which can bring you happiness. Remember: "Enjoy life every moment. Let others enjoy life through you." Pride and dignity are as natural to you as a swan is to water. But enjoy. It is as you want it to be. Reliving the past is negative. Live now. Now is the most important moment in your life. And now is always now. There is not one moment of your past that can compare with the importance of your now. The nows affect and create the realities of the future nows. But again, there is no more important moment than the now. Live it. Enjoy it. Cherish it. It is God's gift to you.*

Enough. I shall give you a key. It shall be yours to always bring you back to love when you stray. It is a thought process that shall be at your fingertips when you want, always there.

Visualize, either in front of you or in your mind, the letters L O V E. *They appear as an object, the four letters as you see them. They are white and flimsy, almost transparent. They blend into one white cloud of energy, and the cloud now enters your body through your heart and gently expands into all of your being, your spirit, your mind; and you experience vibrations and a slight smile. It is on your face and in your eyes, and you feel and generate love. And it shall come to be that even the slightest smile on your face shall trigger the process of love and also the look of love in your eyes. A gentle touch, a pleasant sound, a kind voice, a person you see in need of love. All and any of them shall become a catalyst of feeling your love in your being until you and it become one, forever, for always. It is your key to happiness, no matter what happens around you. Wear it always. Never remove it. Be one with it. With love, I say goodbye to you now. But I am always with you.*

I found Spirit's remarks about living in the "now" most interesting. What moment in time could be more important than the *now,* a moment that connects millions of years of the past to millions of years of the future?

Rasha

One of the most incredible messengers of written Divine guidance from the spirit world is my dear friend Rasha, whom I originally met when I was speaking publicly with an organization called Mind Body Spirit. This organization had put together a group of spiritual speakers who would travel on weekends from one major city to another and give talks to audiences at convention halls and other venues with large capacities. I was one of these speakers for a period of about six months, along with a number of others, some of whom you would likely recognize if I mentioned their names.

One person I developed a friendship with was a very loving, kind, and deeply spiritual woman by the name of Rasha. Several years ago she published a book, which she received and transcribed from *Oneness* over a five-year period. The words are beyond profound, and when reading, you immediately recognize that no human being could have written these words with their conscious mind. (Rasha's Website is: **www.onenesswebsite.com**.)

Rasha has sent me many messages from Oneness over the years, some written to me personally regarding my own life. The following is a direct quotation from the book *Oneness,* transcribed by Rasha, which I know is a message for *you:*

> *These times offer the possibility to transcend the realm of faith based on secondhand experience. These times do not require you to cast your vote based on the spiritual affiliations of your ancestors. These times do not require the commitment of your heart unless your heart is truly in it. You are not being asked to place blind faith in a mode of understanding based on events said to have happened thousands of years back . . . if your own passion has not been kindled by it. These times afford you the opportunity to see for yourself. And then, not simply to believe it . . . but to know it.*
>
> *That is why you have come. That is why you have ventured from the comfort of your own "home" into the wild landscapes this incarnation has provided. This is why you find yourself in a world that no longer seems to make sense. And that is why you look around you and wonder, silently or otherwise, if the world has simply gone mad. For the seeming senselessness of much of the drama that swirls around you is the precursor to the purging that these circumstances cry out for . . . vibrationally, and why the inevitability of change is the order of the day.*
>
> *You have come as the witness . . . and you have come as a participant.*

Although Rasha is American, she's lived the last eight years in India, a country she dearly loves. She feels a great harmony within her when she is there. I suspect she has lived many lifetimes in India.

It was Rasha who introduced me to someone I'm told is one of the holiest men in India. I'll talk about him at the end of the next chapter, but first I'd like to share the experiences I had as a child that prepared me for the present, as well as the future. As I think back to my youth, I realize the tremendous impact these experiences had on me, and how my life would be so different today had I made different choices as I grew older.

Chapter 4

My Background

We all come into this world tremendously influenced by our life experiences. When we're young, growing up in our home environment, there are very few major decisions that we're required to make—the pathway of our journey is narrow and focused. It's when we grow older that we find we come to various crossroads, and we have to decide which direction to take, each choice changing our lives dramatically.

What college do we attend? Do we move from our hometown to another location? Whom do we decide to marry and raise a family with? What occupation do we pursue? If we had chosen a different pathway at any of those crossings, our lives would be substantially different today.

I didn't come from affluence. At the same time, I felt blessed by what I experienced when I was growing up. I feel it is crucial that I share with you my earlier background and what is in my soul, for I'll soon be getting into some very controversial material, and credibility is a very important issue for me.

My Home and Neighborhood

I was born and raised in a suburb of Boston called Chelsea. One of the poorest cities in the country, it is connected to Boston by a bridge that goes over the harbor. If I recall, at that time there were more than 30,000 people living in two square miles. To my knowledge, only one single-family residence (owned by an attorney) existed in Chelsea. On the street where I lived, most of the houses were three stories high, with a family living on each floor; or were built as three-story duplexes, with six families living in them. None of the houses had garages, as they were built in the early 1900s, and very few people owned cars.

In the wintertime, we kids would play tackle football on the streets, the snow acting as our artificial turf, protecting us from injury. In the spring, summer, and fall, we'd nail a rectangular board to a telephone pole, attach the metal band of a barrel rim to it, and create an outdoor basketball court in the street. Oftentimes we couldn't afford a basketball, so we used a tennis ball as a substitute.

My family lived on the first floor of a three-story house, without hot water, and my parents paid $25 a month in rent. My mother would heat a teakettle on the stove in order to put hot water in a cup so that my father could shave. We had one very tiny bathroom off the equally small kitchen, and when we wanted to take a bath, we would fill the water in the tub and let it sit for half an hour, hoping it would reach room temperature. Once I began to play sports in high school, the showers at the high-school gym and stadium locker room became very popular with me.

Our heat was supplied by a coal-burning furnace in the cellar. My father taught me at an early age how to sift the ashes out, shovel coal into the opening, and fight off potential attacks from rats with my shovel. The furnace would burn out in the middle of the night during the winter, so my mother would put my one pair of jeans on the stove to heat them, and then pass them to me under the covers so I could get dressed before I got out of bed, since it would be freezing in our flat.

My Childhood

In spite of our poverty, I *loved* my childhood. The friends I grew up with were like brothers and sisters to me, and they will always have a special place in my heart. We were all mostly first-generation Americans, but the names on our athletic team read like a roster of foreigners thanks to our varied heritages: Italian, Polish, Irish, and many others.

During my junior year in high school, the United Nations even gave us an award at an assembly because our senior class had elected Teddy Chin, who was Chinese, as our class president; Johnny Hagen, who was black, as vice president; and Bobbie Freedman, who was Jewish, as treasurer. We also had an Italian secretary. We were totally puzzled by what the fuss was about, for prejudice didn't seem to exist in our neighborhood.

Although I am forever grateful for my incredible childhood, I always knew that I was different from my friends. Even though profanity was in common use, whenever I swore I would ask under my breath that God forgive me. I was very conscious of not saying any word that would be critical of another. As a high-school student, I was captain of the football team and president of my class one year. At lunchtime in the cafeteria, I recall I'd make a concerted effort to sit with the least popular kids in school, hoping that this would help them with their self-esteem and popularity.

I remember one time my friend Guidi needed a new pair of shoes and had no money. I worked part-time jobs and had a $10 bill on me, which I slipped into the pocket of his jacket, without ever telling him that it came from me.

I'm not sharing these experiences with you because I want to brag, but because I changed later in life, having lost that innocence. I want to give you a picture of what I was like back then.

As a young child, I had a tremendous love for Jeshua, even though he wasn't part of my upbringing. My friends who went to parochial school would sometimes tell me that when my parents died, they would go to hell because they weren't Christians, which is what the students were taught by the priests and nuns. I would often lie in bed at night, telling Jeshua how much I loved him (even though I didn't really know him)—and, with tears coming down my cheeks, I'd beg him not to let my mother and father go to hell.

My Parents

My parents were very special to me. Neither of them had a high-school education, and my father often worked two jobs, one in a factory and one as a night watchman, in order to pay the rent and put food on our table.

I can recall one day when my father came home from work, and my mother asked him if she could have some money to buy food for dinner. My father told her that he'd had $10, but he'd given it to the widow next door to feed her children, since she had no money. My mother went up to my father and hugged him and told him he'd done the right thing. I learned the meaning of generosity from them.

My sister often told me that our mother had certain psychic abilities. For instance, Mom might say that a friend of my sister's was pregnant a day before the friend herself called with the good news. Or my mother would state that somebody who was looking for a job would be hired the next day, and he or she would.

Mom told me that when she gave birth to my older brother, he was very ill and everyone thought he was going to die that first day. That evening at the hospital her deceased father had appeared, sitting in the chair next to her bed, and assured her that my brother would survive. He also told Mom that he loved her and he was fine.

My mother suffered from Alzheimer's during the last few years of her life. She had been the youngest of seven children and was the only one in her family who was still alive at that point. My father and sister cared for her during those years and witnessed many wondrous things.

At times my mother would be facing a blank wall, talking in a language no one understood. When my father and sister asked who she was talking to, sometimes she'd reply that it was her mother or give the name of one of her deceased siblings. My sister said it was apparent to her that at times our mother's spirit was not in her body—it would leave and come back several times a day. My mom would tell my sister that she had been visiting her family. It was very beautiful where they were, she explained, and they wanted her to join them, but she wasn't ready to leave my sister and father yet.

One day my father got a phone call with the news that my older cousin Mike was very ill in the hospital. He and my sister agreed not to discuss this in front of my mother, for they weren't sure what she could understand. Later that day Mom had one of those conversations with invisible people, and when she was through, she informed my sister that her deceased sister Dora, who was Mike's mother, had told her that Mike was in the hospital and she was worried about him. These are just some of my family's incredible stories.

I remember the last time I saw my mother before she passed away. I was visiting her at home in Chelsea, and although I'd been there for three days, she still hadn't recognized me. On my last day, I knelt in front of her as she sat in her wheelchair. Her eyes weren't focused, and I knew she couldn't see me. I said to her, "Mom, it's me, Nick."

She lifted her chin and looked at me. Her eyes came into focus, and she smiled. She extended her arms out to me, her hands shaking. She looked at me for five seconds, and the last words I ever heard her say were: "Nick, Nick, God is so good to me."

For many years I couldn't tell that story without shedding tears (as I am now) for the fact that despite her debilitating sickness, she could thank God for letting her see me for those five precious seconds.

My parents were not sophisticated or educated, but they were the kindest and most generous and loving people I have ever met in my life. I cry even now as I write these words, feeling sorry that I didn't tell them often enough how much I loved and respected them.

The greatest enjoyment my father had was watching me participate in sports. In addition to being the captain of the football team, making some of the all-state teams, I played basketball and ran track. I was also an honor student, although my high school had one of the lowest academic ratings in the country.

I had football-scholarship offers from many colleges, some of them Ivy League schools. But with the wisdom of a 17-year-old kid from the ghetto, I accepted the one that enabled me to never have to ask my folks for a cent during those four years, from a school in the South that excelled in sports: the University of Florida.

My Spirituality

As a youngster, I felt a spiritual power within me, a feeling that I had a responsibility to live in a manner that was beyond reproach. I continued to have this feeling through college . . . but then I began to lose it when I later joined the military.

I was an officer in the Army, and because of my college athletic background, I was eventually made second in command of 1,700 men in an elite organization called Special Troops. It was in that position that I learned how to become an effective public speaker and leader. Many times I had to give talks to the soldiers in an auditorium—on subjects such as hygiene, escape and evasion from the enemy, first aid, and how to conduct oneself if one became a prisoner of war. It was how I began to develop a tougher demeanor, a thicker skin, so to speak. This expanded even further when I went into the business world.

I asked Spirit one day why I had changed so much. What happened to that purity I'd once felt within my soul? Spirit answered me by saying that I still had my same sensitivities, but I needed to have these experiences in order to be toughened up in preparation for what lay ahead of me. To this day, I still cry when I read about an earthquake killing innocent people in another part of the world, or a family grieving over the loss of a child in a car accident.

But I never consider myself to be someone special. Even today, knowing and believing in my past incarnation as Paul, when I'm asked if I think I'm better or more important than other people, the answer is no. Just as I'm not offended if someone chooses to think I'm a fraud or insane or living an illusion, neither do I place myself on any pedestal for those who do accept my past incarnation, or who try to show me special attention or respect. I don't ask for that, nor do I seek it. You—and every person on this planet—have had past lives, some of which I'm sure were also very profound, and we are all equal in God's eyes.

I don't believe that *I* am particularly important, but the messages I share with you are. I think of myself as a messenger of God and of Jeshua. I have no fear of the mission before me. I'm grateful that I don't have any anxieties, for I am well aware of the challenges I face. But I also know that God and my spiritual advisors and guides are with me and are supporting my efforts.

I've mentioned that five highly evolved people shared the news of my forthcoming mission with me. Rasha was one such person, and she introduced me to another, Dr. Bindu Purohit, a holy man from India. (The others were John Lawrence, whom I mentioned in the Introduction; Janet, an angel mystic I'll talk about in Part III; and Laurie McQuary, whom you'll meet in Part II.)

Rasha has told me of miracles she has seen Dr. Bindu perform. It is my understanding that people come from all over the world to get an audience with him for ten minutes.

Dr. Bindu is the 13th-generation descendant of a lineage known as "Raj Gurus." These holy men have acted as spiritual mentors to the high gurus and royal families of India throughout the ages. His work is based on an ancient spiritual science that can alter the structure of material reality through sound vibration and prayer. The final goal of this sacred art is to empower people to become one with what he refers to as the "Supreme Divine Power."

I feel blessed that the last three times he's been to the U.S., Dr. Bindu has asked me to meet him at the modest house where he stays, which sits on the bay in Sausalito, a short distance north of San Francisco over the Golden Gate Bridge. On these occasions, we've spent four or five hours together, with Dr. Bindu sitting on a sofa in a lotus position, wearing a native Indian outfit that appeared to be made of silk, cut somewhat like pajamas (which I understand is referred to as a *lungi*).

It has always been quite an experience being with him. He has shared many spiritual thoughts with me, including the role of spirit guides in our lives. He has talked about how we are influenced by our past-life experiences and are dealing with both the negative and positive karma that we accumulate from them.

The last time we met, Dr. Bindu asked me if I wondered why he had taken such an interest in me.

"Why?" I prompted.

He responded by telling me that I would become a spiritual leader in the world, and that he wanted to help me when it was time. He told me that I would be meeting with the Pope in the future—although there would be difficult times with the current one, Benedict XVI, I would have a very close friendship with the next Pope.

I accepted his words with gratitude but not surprise. At that time he was the third of the seers who had heralded my mission.

What I've found of great interest is that most of these highly evolved souls do not practice a religion. They all have a spiritual relationship with God that is intensely personal and marked by great intimacy. This is true of both Rasha and others who are very ascended individuals (whom you will meet in the pages of this book).

I have come to believe that religion provides us with a vehicle —a very important one—that allows us to traverse the "mountain," at the top of which is God. But at some point as we come closer to the peak, we will abandon the vehicle—religion—and will continue the journey on foot to reach the summit, to be at one with God.

But as you can see, religion plays a vital part in this journey. It can take you to that point on the mountain where you can continue on your own. Having said that, though, the Christian religion must carry with it the true messages of Jeshua and Paul, and teach universal love and compassion—not fear and guilt—and not be used to polarize people, which leads to suffering, hostility, and wars. And the purpose of *Time for Truth*, which I will reiterate several times, is not to try to hurt or destroy Christianity, but to give it a new beginning . . . and it can happen with your help.

Now it is time to move on to an extraordinary experience I want to tell you about. It is one I'll always remember, another Divine intervention that has reminded me of my mission.

Chapter 5

THE SACRED BIRDS

Something extraordinary took place in my life in the early winter of 1995. I wrote about the two incidents in this chapter and then sent the story to my six "test readers," who also function as my sounding boards. They come from different parts of the world: three are outside of the U.S., one is from Memphis, and two live in my city in Oregon. (I'll introduce them in the Acknowledgments at the end of the book.) They suggested when I should elaborate and noted when I'd gone into too much detail. Sometimes I agreed with them, and sometimes I didn't.

This time I got several different opinions as to whether I should include this story in the book. The main issue was: how do I tell it without being viewed as self-important? It caused me great concern.

One colleague advised me to leave the chapter out. Another said, "Your book is called *Time for Truth,* and the story is true, so you can't leave it out." Yet another suggested that I share what I'm feeling and my reservations, as I just have, and then let the story speak for itself.

You and I have been together now for a while. We are no longer strangers to one another. In many ways, you know me better than any friend or member of my family, for I've shared things with you that I never have with them or anybody else before. One person may have known parts of some of my stories, another some other parts, and so on—but I've never before told anyone *all* the things I'm discussing here. At this point, I'm hoping we have bonded enough for you to appreciate the wonder of this story.

The Lake Experience

Whenever I think of miracles, I cannot help but remember the incredible event that took place on the lake adjacent to my backyard. I remember every detail as if it happened yesterday.

The lake is about three miles long, and the width between my back property and the land on the other side is about 400 yards. It's a private lake only used by the approximately 300 homeowners along the shore. My house sits on a bluff about 30 feet above the water.

One late Sunday afternoon, my friend Thomas was visiting me from out of town. The two of us were playing backgammon at my kitchen table, which enjoyed a view of the lake from floor-to-ceiling windows. It was an overcast day, with dark clouds covering the entire sky.

At one point, Thomas looked out the window and called my attention to the hundreds of birds landing on the water directly adjacent to my property. We watched for a while and were amazed that the birds just kept coming from every direction—north, south, east, and west—as well as the sky above. We decided to go outside and witness this phenomenon.

It had now gotten dark, and because of the cloud cover, the moon and stars weren't visible. There must have been thousands of birds congregating, yet I'd never seen this species on the lake before. They were white and small, and although I wasn't close enough to tell for sure, they very well could have been doves. Then several began making a loud bird noise—and, as if on cue, all of them began to chirp and shriek in unison.

Thomas and I looked at each other, baffled. We both raised our arms in the air, wide apart, like Moses trying to part the Red Sea; and the birds responded by immediately becoming silent. I don't know why we made that gesture. It was almost instinctive, but my friend and I knew for sure that something of an extraordinary spiritual nature was occurring right before us.

Then three very large bands of light appeared on the water, connecting the shoreline of my yard and the other side of the lake, cutting a path directly across the birds. The band in the middle was reddish orange, and I would guess about 14 feet in width. The two on either side of it were a golden orange color, each approximately ten feet wide. What was so incredible was that there was absolutely nothing that could be creating these bands of light. On the opposite shore was a very steep, undeveloped hillside. There were no homes or streetlights or any other sources of light that could have cast those colored reflections onto the lake.

While Thomas and I stood on my deck observing this incredible sight, something took place immediately above our heads that I can't explain. It was as if some very large, invisible bird was hovering just a few feet above and was rapidly moving its wings, creating a loud *whooshing* noise. Both Thomas and I looked up, startled, but we couldn't see anything. There was no roof over our heads, only a dark sky, but the whooshing noise continued for about five or six seconds. When it stopped, my friend looked at me and quietly said, "Nick, it must be angels." About ten minutes later the whooshing was repeated, and again we couldn't see anything that would be responsible for those sounds.

Thomas and I stood on the deck watching the scene before us for another two hours. (My wife came home and joined us for the last hour.) There was a calmness and serenity that is almost impossible to describe. When it was finally time to call it a night, I drove Thomas to the hotel where he was staying, which was about 15 minutes away. The birds were still resting on the lake when I returned, but they were gone the next morning.

The Birds Return

One week later, I was preparing to pick up a friend because we had tickets to a basketball game. My child's nanny was tidying up in the family room when she called my name. She pointed out that something unusual was happening on the lake: once again, hundreds and hundreds of birds were in the exact same place where they'd landed one week earlier. They were the same species, and again came from all directions. It was a clear day, so I ran for my camera to photograph what was taking place.

Soon all the birds had arrived, once more appearing to number over 2,000. All of a sudden, as I stood on the deck watching them, they began to make their shrieking bird noises in unison, as they had the week before. After a while I raised my arms and began to softly pray, and when I did, the birds became totally silent.

I don't know how long I stood there on the deck, quietly praying and talking to my guides and angels. I lost track of time and was filled with a sense of peace and tranquility, as if I were in a state of bliss.

Finally, I realized it was time for me to leave or I'd be late for the game, so I turned and started to open the French doors to reenter the family room. As I did so, I heard an incredible noise coming from the lake. The birds had left the surface and were in a frenzy, flying in total chaos, shrieking loudly again. This went on for about 30 seconds as I snapped some photos of this amazing scene.

I then raised my arms, as I had before, and began praying, and the birds immediately returned to the surface of the lake and sat there in total silence. My feeling at that moment could best be described as awe. The atmosphere of the scene was sacred.

As I have shared with you earlier, there are many different ways in which Spirit can intervene in our lives. Based on what I had just witnessed, there wasn't any doubt in my mind regarding the purpose of the birds as they related to me. I felt that their coming from all different directions represented people from the four corners of the world. Their dovelike appearance and color represented humanity's hope for universal peace and love. And even when the birds went into a frenzy, inside of me was this intense understanding that they thought I was abandoning them, turning my back on them—that I was not going to live up to my commitment to my mission for the sake of my brothers and sisters around the world.

I've mentioned the birds to a number of my friends in the neighborhood, including some who grew up on the lake and have lived there as long as 40 years. They all said the same thing: they had never, ever seen those birds. And *I* have never seen them again either, since that day.

I am providing you with three photos of the birds:

The birds coming from all different directions, landing on the lake.

The birds settled quietly on the lake.

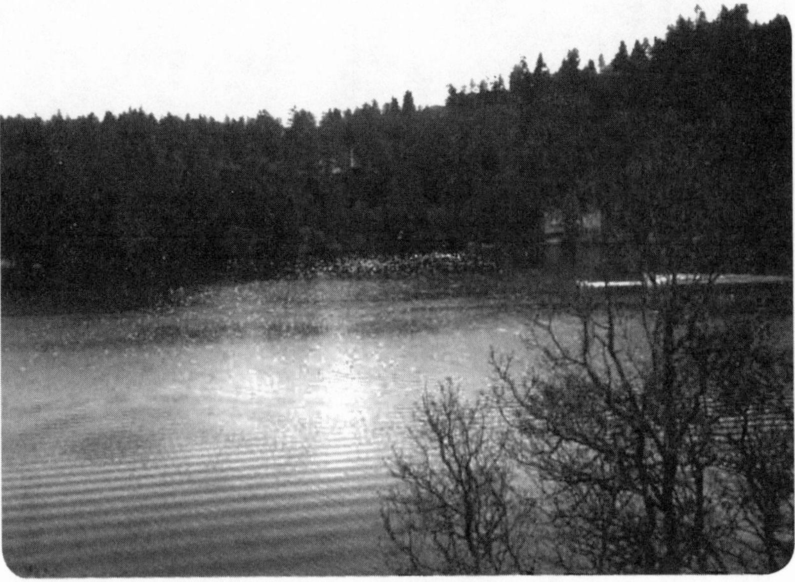

The birds swarming in a frenzy when I turned my back on them to leave.

As I mentioned, I'm creating a Website for readers (which I'll talk about in the Contact the Author section at the end of this book). In addition to many other activities, such as sharing 444 experiences, there is an area where you can express your comments and reactions to the events I've described in this chapter, as well as other topics in this book. I would truly love to hear what you have to say.

In the next chapter, I'll share another way in which Divine intervention can manifest. I hope you're enjoying this journey so far. Please join me as I relate another story filled with miracles.

Chapter 6

God's Healer

The story in this chapter involves two people who I believe are the epitome of living saints: Sara O'Meara and Yvonne Fedderson. Through their foundation for severely abused children, Childhelp, they have saved the lives of more than five million young people desperately in need of assistance. They have also been nominated four years in a row for the Nobel Peace Prize.

As you read their story, you will discover how God intervened in their lives. Remember that Divine intervention doesn't have to be confined to just a single event or a series of events—it can also alter the entire direction of a person's life, as it did theirs.

A Miraculous Healing

In 1971, Sara had been diagnosed with terminal cancer. In February of 1972, she was told she had three months to live, as the cancer had spread through her entire body. While lying in her hospital bed watching TV, an evangelist by the name of Kathryn Kuhlman appeared on the screen and told viewers to come to the Shrine Auditorium in Los Angeles to see God perform miracles.

In spite of a fresh incision that ran from underneath her earlobe down to her upper thigh, Sara was able to persuade the doctors to allow her to attend the service. They felt that since she was dying anyway, what was the difference?

A friend of Sara's took her to the auditorium, and only one seat was still available when she arrived, on the farthest aisle of the first row of the highest balcony. During the presentation, Kathryn stopped and looked up at Sara. She told the audience that there was a woman in a red dress seated in the upper balcony who was dying of cancer, but that God was going to perform a miracle and heal her now. She said the woman would know she was being healed, for it would feel like a thousand needles were going through her body at that instant. Sara stated that the energy was so powerful that it knocked everyone next to her sideways, like a domino effect.

Sara was asked to walk down to the stage and give a testimonial, which she did. When she got home, she saw further evidence of the miracle. She examined her body and found that her skin had healed completely, covering her stitches and the clamps that kept the large incision closed. When the doctor examined her the next day, his face turned white, and then he ran out of the room to tell others of this miracle.

Sara and Yvonne both became assistants to Kathryn, helping her with her presentations at the Shrine Auditorium and on her TV show. Several years later, Kathryn invited them to join her for a trip to the Holy Land. While there, she told Sara that God had now given *her* the ability to pray for people while the Lord healed them. Weeks later, Kathryn's soul had a transition and God called her home. Soon after, Sara discovered that indeed God had chosen her to replace Kathryn as a healer, and she started on an incredible journey, filled with many miracles.

Serendipity in Scottsdale

I met Sara and Yvonne on a beautiful night in 1997. I was giving a symposium at an outdoor facility in Scottsdale, Arizona, with more than a thousand people in attendance. There was a TV crew that filmed my three-hour presentation, which was later featured in a 30-minute segment on a weekly national show. Following the presentation, while I was signing copies of *The Messengers* for those in the audience, seven or eight people independently told me that they had witnessed an amazing thing taking place while I was onstage. They said that as I was talking, a green mist had come out of my mouth, and green balls had formed and floated around me. I learned later that green is the color of healing.

That was the night Sara and Yvonne introduced themselves to me and invited me to join them for lunch at their home the next day. The two of them and their husbands had purchased a very large home that they shared on six acres of land in the Greater Phoenix area, and they'd built a beautiful chapel on their property. Once a month they held a nondenominational service, which always concluded with Sara doing a healing for those in the audience who were in need. I was invited to attend the next service, as well as to be a guest speaker.

When I arrived at the chapel for the service, I noticed a tall, thin black man in a light tan suit standing outside. He had a beautiful smile on his face, even though he seemed quite nervous as he greeted people, and I wondered who he was.

He was there, I soon learned, to share the story of his own miracle. At the end of the service, Sara invited the man onto the stage to tell the audience his story. This is what he told us:

> Five years earlier he had been working in Los Angeles for a major hotel. His job was to be the chauffeur for guests who were considered VIPs and drive them wherever they wished to be taken. He was in very bad health at the time and was severely crippled. He weighed well over 300 pounds, and his doctors had ordered a special wheelchair made for him because of his size.
>
> He said he hadn't known the identities of the two ladies he had been driving around, but on the second day, Sara, who was in the backseat with Yvonne, tapped him on the shoulder and asked him if he was ready to have

God perform a healing on him so he could walk normally. He was dumbfounded by the question, and when asked a second time, he said, "Sure."

Sara began to pray for him as he sat behind the wheel. Then she told him that God had healed him, and instructed him to get out of the car and walk.

He obeyed and tried to walk, but in his crippled style (which he imitated for us in the chapel). Sara then said, with authority in her voice, "No, walk normal. God has healed you."

The man looked at the audience with tears in his eyes, and began to leap in the air and dance on the stage, shouting that God had healed him. He told of how he had gone back to the hospital and the doctors couldn't believe what had happened to him. They made him come back week after week so other doctors could look at his x-rays and see evidence of the healing he had experienced that day.

I am shedding tears of joy now as I am writing these words, as I did when I heard this man's story that afternoon in 1997.

Over the years I have seen God perform many miracles through my friend Sara. I have seen people get up from wheelchairs and walk who hadn't walked in years. I have seen people healed of cancer, diabetes, and all kinds of different diseases. This brings to mind what happened at another service of hers I attended.

When Sara came onstage, she announced to the audience that God had told her that there were five people in attendance that day who had cancer. She asked if they would raise their hands and be identified.

Not one raised his or her hand. I suppose everyone was embarrassed to do so. Sara asked again, and again no one moved.

Sara said, "All right," and stepped down from the stage and began to walk down the middle aisle that divided the audience of approximately 125 people. She stopped at the fourth row, looked to her right, and said that God was telling her that there was a woman in that row with cancer who came for a healing, and would she please raise her hand? The woman immediately did.

Then Sara took a few more steps, looked to her left, and said that God was telling her that there was a man in that row who had come for the same purpose; and he raised *his* hand. One by one, Sara identified all five of the individuals in question and then prayed for a healing for them. I don't know if those people were in fact healed, but I've been a witness as hundreds and hundreds of others *have* been healed in the same manner. Some are even restored to health as they're driving to the chapel, before they arrive at the service.

This isn't the case for every person Sara prays for. She and I have discussed several times why it is that some are healed and some are not. Sara has said repeatedly that she isn't the one doing the healing; God is. Therefore, it's the Lord's call as to who is the beneficiary.

But we do know that when people are healed, they're healed permanently—it's not just a temporary effect, perhaps due to some function of their minds. For example, Sara prayed for a teenager who had one leg shorter than the other by several inches . . . and instantly both legs became the same length. The only explanation is that a miracle occurred, and there have been so many others like it.

As I've told Sara, I don't know where her gifts from God begin and end. I do truly believe that she and Yvonne are living saints, perhaps in their last incarnation on Earth. In addition to the gifts of healing, they still continue to dedicate themselves to humanitarian and spiritual causes.

A Healing Mission

Our spirit guides informed Sara and me that someday we'd be doing symposiums together in the U.S. and abroad and would be touching the lives of millions of people. We were told that at the end of each presentation, I would do a spiritual healing (which I will share with you in a later chapter), and then Sara would pray for physical healings.

Sara and I, with the help of Yvonne, do plan to give these presentations all over. As I wrote earlier, I was told by five different seers, very evolved people who didn't even know each other (apart from Rasha and Dr. Bindu), that she and I would be doing just that: traveling around the world as spiritual teachers. Previously, I hadn't been sure how this was to come about, but I knew that there had to be some catalyst. You just don't one day decide that you're going to be a spiritual leader in the world.

Then about two years ago I was contacted by a very talented Hollywood scriptwriter who had read *The Messengers*. She asked me if we could work together to create a screenplay. We agreed to do so, with her doing most of the creative work and me acting as the theological source and helping with the editing. The result was a wonderful screenplay. It incorporated my personal story, including my past-life-regression sessions, and another plot that takes place in the Vatican. The two plots become intertwined halfway through. We loved the story but weren't successful in getting it into the hands of a Hollywood producer or director.

I'd hoped the movie would be the catalyst enabling Sara and me to begin our mission, as described by the five seers. But when that didn't happen, it was then that I had the 444 experiences (including my bedside lamp going on at 4:44 A.M., as described in the Introduction) that led me to write this book.

I'm assuming that *Time for Truth* will be the catalyst, and someday you'll be able to witness Sara's healings in person. I say this because without a book or a movie to make the public aware of these messages and Sara's gifts, a speaking mission isn't possible. It's the difference between having 50 people in your audience and having several thousand.

It is all in God's hands. Whatever is in store for us, Sara, Yvonne, and I are ready to be God's messengers. In preparation for our work, I've formed a nonprofit corporation called The Great Tomorrow, a spiritual foundation committed to providing hope that there is a better life ahead of us, and promoting universal love and compassion for God's children.

I truly believe that there are many thousands who also feel God's spirit inside of their own souls, and that most likely *you* have experienced a stirring of your spirit—something that you feel inside of you, in your soul, but perhaps cannot describe. I hope you will become a part of our efforts to create a new beginning in the world, a truly Great Tomorrow.

Moving Forward

While writing *Time for Truth,* I occasionally questioned whether I would be able to justify the burdens and exposure inherent in placing myself in such a sensitive position. There were times I asked myself why I should take on the responsibility of trying to correct the mistruths that have affected the lives of people for more than 1,600 years. The challenges are great, and the rewards are hard to define.

Not too long ago while sitting at my desk, I was instructed by Spirit to write down a message they wanted to give me. This is what they said:

> *Nick, you must believe in yourself at all times. You must never lose faith that you are capable of accomplishing anything in life you choose to do. And you must always choose the highest good. It is not enough for you to choose to achieve excellence. For you must believe in yourself enough to accomplish that which others cannot accomplish.*
>
> *To believe in yourself, you must have the courage that exceeds the need for the consideration of courage. It must be a natural part of your life that avoids any need for decision making based on* <u>*whether*</u> *you have the courage to do that which you must. This must be a belief beyond personal questioning, beyond personal doubt, to a point where it can no longer be considered a matter of courage, but rather a way of life. That shall be so, for you will believe in yourself.*
>
> *You must have character that is beyond criticism and is a permanent part of yourself. It is not imagined or pretended. Every moment of your life must be naturally conducted with pride and dignity that cannot be confused with arrogance, but recognized with respect.*

Your character must always contain compassion and concern for others. This concern will be genuine, for you will never lose sight of your humble background in trying to understand those you have difficulty in identifying with, for they are the majority of the world and the ones who need help the most.

You must believe in yourself so that your character never bends, never compromises, and is consistent. You must believe in your intellect—that no task is beyond your ability. Your intellect is a gift that you shall not waste, and you shall use it to its greatest capacity. You must have the patience and tolerance to realize that others will not always agree with you or understand you. But rather than find fault, you shall try harder to reach them, for it shall become your responsibility to serve them. This is your calling. You cannot question it. You must accept it.

I have read the preceding words many times since they were given to me, and they have had a great impact on me. And Spirit is correct: these words have become a way of life for me. They are my code of conduct . . . and I invite you to accept them as yours as well, if you so choose.

There are many other things I want to share with you. My mind is fighting itself to find some order, some sequence, and some continuity of information that will make sense. There is an energy inside and around me almost demanding that I look for, find, and press a magic button. But there is no magic button. And you are reading these words long after I wrote them, so apparently God and my guides did assist in putting these thoughts in some order that enabled them to be published and made available to you.

So now let us move forward in our journey to find the truth. Together, we will delve into the heart of it all: *What is the purpose of our lives?* and *What is our relationship with God?*

Let's go for it!

PART II

THE SPIRITUAL WORLD

Introduction to Part II

An elderly African man in sandals wearing gray shorts and a sleeveless white shirt stands in the sand along the ocean's shore, water cresting at his feet. It is evening, and there are thousands of stars in the sky. He looks toward the heavens, his heart heavy, and he is filled with wonder. He asks, "Dear God, what is the purpose of my life?"

A petite middle-aged Asian woman dressed in a simple white robe sits yoga-style on a quiet mountaintop. She looks at the horizon in all directions, then at the sky above. Her emotions are serene, and she is filled with hope. She asks, "Dear Lord, what is my relationship with You?"

These two questions have been asked since the beginning of time, in countries and societies worldwide. Throughout history, people from every corner of the earth, from every ethnic background and walk of life—presidents of companies and migrant laborers alike—have all wondered: *What is the purpose of my life?* and *What is my relationship with God?*

I have spent many years seeking the answers to those questions. Some of the information I've found comes from extensive research. Other truths have arisen from discussions with several of the most highly evolved people on the planet, and I'm sharing a few of their stories with you in this book. Some of the knowledge has come directly from Spirit, communicated through the gift of channeled writing, and some through six months of hypnotic regression in which I accessed the memory of one who had walked with Jeshua 2,000 years ago. And last, on occasion I have received information through the gift of claircognizance, transmitted to my mind telepathically by my spirit guides.

I'm not going to ask you to wait until Chapter 10 or 20 to learn the purpose of your life and the nature of your relationship with God. I will share the answers to these questions with you now, and I will address both of them together . . . for they are interconnected and cannot be separated.

Sixteen hundred years ago, the premedieval Roman Universal (Catholic) Church took the position that you can only find God through *it.* You are out there on the left, God is way over there on the right, and the Church is in the middle. The Church taught that indeed it is the conduit between you and God. Without the house of worship or religion, you cannot have God, and there is no salvation or redemption.

But the truth is, you are part of God and God is part of you. The spirit of God is inside you. That is why you are eternal and immortal. That is why you are not a human being who by coincidence has a spirit and soul; you are a spirit with a soul who is having a human experience. You don't need someone else to help you find God, for again, God is quite literally inside of you. Having a part of the Lord's spirit is what gives you life. This is what Jeshua meant when he preached 2,000 years ago that the kingdom of heaven is within you.

So if this is the case, how do you interface and interact with God? How do you become at one with God? The information I'm going to share with you has been provided to me by Divine sources that I refer to as *Oneness,* which is a collective of God, Jeshua, and your angels and spirit guides.

Stairway to Ascension

Visualize a pyramid of a thousand steps inside you, and at the very top is God and Christ Consciousness. The purpose of your life is to climb the steps, one at a time, until you reach the top and become at one with God and achieve Christ Consciousness, which means that you have become as Jeshua was. You're not just a part of God—you have become *at one* with God. You've evolved to the highest level possible.

You proceed up the steps of the pyramid by embracing universal love and compassion and living in truth in your everyday life. That is how you *ascend.* And obviously many people can also *descend* the steps—remove themselves further from becoming at one with God by living in a mode that is the opposite of expressing love and compassion to others.

But you may wonder: *What if I don't reach the top during this lifetime?* For in reality, most people can only raise their ascension, their evolvement, a few steps at a time. Yes, it takes many lifetimes to reach the top.

When you were a child and completed the fourth grade, you took time off in the summer to regroup and to prepare to continue your education in the fall. And when you returned to school in August or September, you didn't advance from a fourth grader to a junior in high school or a senior in college. You came back to continue at the place you left off, and you began the first day of the fifth grade.

The same is true in the spiritual world. If the transition of your soul from your body (death) occurred when you were on your 320th step, that is where you shall begin when reincarnated in your next journey through life.

Each of us is on a different step depending on how highly we have evolved. In my pyramid analogy, masters would be at the equivalent of their 700th step, while living saints would be in the high 800s and 900s. The average person is at around step 200, which is very sad, for those below this point are always obsessed with negative preoccupations such as anger, revenge, jealousy, greed, selfishness, guilt, or fear.

The reason we have terrorism in the world is because there are so many people who are filled with fear, but rather than acknowledge it, they prefer converting it into hatred. They direct this emotion toward those they hold responsible for causing that fear, therefore justifying their acts of hatred. If we were able to eliminate their fear, we could erase their hatred—as well as terrorism—from the world.

The Purpose of Reincarnation

Without the gift of reincarnation, you would never be able to reach the top of the pyramid. If you had only one life to live, as insisted upon by the Catholic Church, there's no way you could become at one with God. For example, what happens, based on the teachings of the Church, to the spirit of a child who dies very young in an accident? Or that of a baby who dies shortly after birth? Apparently the Church would have you believe they remain as children forever, with the same mind and conceptual understanding, since they would never mature to adulthood or be able to distinguish right from wrong.

I attended a Catholic Mass one night with my wife, and the priest told those in attendance that when children die, they go to purgatory. He said he didn't know what "purgatory" meant, but it was probably someplace between heaven and hell. *Someplace between heaven and hell?* Can you imagine a million babies in purgatory? Who cares for them? Who has diaper duty?

The truth is that 2,000 years ago, Jeshua, as well as most of the Jewish people, believed in reincarnation. This is also true of the religious leaders for the first several hundred years after the birth of Christianity. (I will share details of this in Part III of this book.)

So, to summarize, your purpose in life is to become at one with God by ascending the stairs of the pyramid, by living your life embracing universal love and universal compassion. And your relationship with your Higher Power is one in which you are an eternal and immortal child of God, and God's spirit resides within you.

In Part II, we'll continue to explore a number of questions related to the spiritual world: *What is our relationship with our spirit guides and angels? What is the purpose of reincarnation? Are our lives predetermined?* as well as many others. In the next chapter, we'll begin by examining our relationship with the entities in the spiritual realm.

Chapter 7

Spirit Guides and Angels

We are constantly given information by the spiritual realm, a source we all have available to us, even if very few realize this or know how to access spiritual knowledge.

Although you may not believe at this moment that there is a spiritual world that is constantly monitoring your life, inspiring you and encouraging you when you're in need of help, it is my sincere hope that you will be a believer once you've finished *Time for Truth.*

Let's Talk

In this chapter I want to discuss spirit guides. But before I do, I'd like to talk to you for a while and share some of the feelings I'm experiencing as I'm writing this book. It's very different from speaking in front of a live audience.

I've only written three books, the last one years ago, but I've probably spoken in front of live audiences more than a hundred times. And even though I might be sharing the same information with both my reading audience and a live one, I have no idea how it is impacting you, the reader.

When I'm in front of an audience, I can feel people's energy. I can read their body language. I can see if they're bored or sitting attentively, absorbing each thought and idea.

With an audience, I can ask whether anyone wants me to repeat any information. I can ask how many, by a show of hands, agree with a position I've taken—and how many are offended. I remember giving a presentation one evening—I don't remember which city I was in—and I was in the middle of telling the audience that they weren't sinners and weren't responsible for Jeshua's death. That's when a middle-aged man and woman sitting to my left got up and began to pass through the row to get to the aisle to leave. They looked slightly embarrassed to be doing so, but at the same time they seemed very upset. Their departure was so abrupt that it took me by surprise, and I felt it would be best if I stopped talking until they'd left the auditorium. However, that was the only time someone walked out of one of my presentations.

But now as I write, I'm realizing that I have no idea how many of you, my readers, may have "walked out"—that is, you stopped reading, or maybe you even threw this book away. Nor do I know how many haven't wanted to put it down, or even pause for a break. I can look out at an audience and see that there may be 5,000 people listening to my words. But if there are the same number of you reading this book at this moment, I don't know if 2,000 of you have called a friend and suggested that they also read it; or if 3,000 have said, "No more," "I'm offended," or "I don't believe what he's writing."

In front of an audience, I can speak louder to make a point. I can speak softer to make members listen with more attention. I can get emotional with them and feel their energy. But as a writer, I don't have the luxury of doing any of those things. Sure, I can type faster or slower, but it is *you* who controls the time we spend together and how often we meet.

I don't know if you're reading on a couch, in bed, or in a chair. As for me, I'm in my family room, sitting at a desk with my computer in front of me. My desk is up against a window with a view overlooking the beautiful lake where I had the miraculous experience I told you about in Chapter 5. I'm currently wearing black sweatpants, a pale blue short-sleeved jersey, and white athletic socks with no shoes. I also have a one-day growth of beard. My picture is on the back cover of the book, so you can envision me, if you choose to, as you read my words.

I wish I could envision *you* to the same degree. I love my audiences, for it is from them that I get my energy, my motivation to speak the truth. To be perfectly candid, I'd rather speak in front of 10,000 people than 5. I wish by some magic I knew how many of you at this very moment are reading my words. Not tomorrow or the day after or yesterday, but *right at this moment.* Would you please raise your hands so I can count you?

What has made me think these thoughts is that, in many ways, I believe this is how our spirit guides feel. They know we can't ordinarily see or hear them. They know that many of us don't even know that they're with us, trying to inspire us when we're down, motivate us when we're without ambition, and help us find our way when we feel lost. They love us and are committed to us beyond words. Their dedication to us is beyond any loyalty we have ever experienced. And yet, they are aware that most of us don't even know they exist.

But exist they do. They are part of *Oneness.* They are God's emissaries.

Spirit Communication

You may have noticed that I often say I was told something by "Spirit," which is how I refer to the spiritual world collectively. Imagine several spiritual entities sitting around a conference table in their dimension. Perhaps they're discussing a problem that you're having, trying to determine how they may be of help to you, what guidance or advice to provide you. Once they've made that decision, they must also decide what means should be used to transfer this information to you.

When the Canadian businessman I told you about in Chapter 1 was awakened in his Geneva hotel room at 4:44 A.M., looked at his clock, and was compelled to call me, was it just one spirit guide having him do these things, or two or three? Were they *his* guides or mine? I truly don't know, but I *do* know he wouldn't have taken those actions without spiritual guidance.

I have been told by Spirit that our guides have previously lived human lives. In one case, my guide many years ago identified himself to me as Z.O. in written channeling. He informed me that he hadn't lived on Earth in more than 500 years and was a very advanced master spirit. At one time I had another guide who identified herself as X.Q., and her energy was much different from that of Z.O.—more casual and feminine. When you're able to personalize your relationship with your guides, you'll be able to formulate your own opinions.

But indeed, your spirit guides are the link between you and divinity. And my goal is to help you find a way to receive communication from them. You see, there is no problem with you communicating to *them*. They can hear your words when you talk to them, whether it be out loud in prayer or silently in meditation. But they also want you to be able to receive *their* words.

In a later chapter, I'm going to try to help you open that door, to be able to dial their number and find the right channel. They have so much they want to share with you. But I *will* give you a message they have for you right now. Please understand that I am not the one creating these words, for I don't have that sort of talent. With everything that is sacred to me, I swear to you—these words are not mine but are coming to you from Spirit, from part of Oneness:

> *As you become engulfed in external matters that are foreign to your soul identity, you lose your perspective of what is really important in life—that is, eternal life. Your very being, your mind, and your personality are perpetual and everlasting. Therefore, your soul is not temporal, and it truly should be that which is of greatest concern to you. Yet, oftentimes your energy focuses on that which is temporal and cannot bring you happiness, peace of mind, or peace of heart.*

Your talents, your creativity, your need to be loved and accepted . . . are all within you. Everything that you seek, in trying to understand your relationship with God, lies within you. For within you is a store that contains many wonderful things. Each of you has a key that will open the door to that store. You may enter it and take what is yours and visit it as often as you choose to, once you understand that it is a gift you have received for being part of God, and inside of you there is a wisdom and spiritual mind that you refrain from trying to communicate with.

Yes, it is difficult to center yourself into your spiritual mind so that you can be in tune with it. But if you are not aware of it—or at best, if you are not making an effort to be in touch with it—it is impossible to become at one with it. Being at one with it brings happiness and understanding, for it shall become obvious to you that there are so many things you worry about in life that are not material, for they have nothing to do with happiness.

So you must look within, for the greatest gifts that you have are internal. You must learn to center yourself. You must learn to find your soul mind. It is there for you to share, and find peace. If you open a channel, you shall see and understand, for it is within every one of God's children.

I truly hope that you will carefully read the preceding words and embrace them. They were meant for *you*. This is your personal message from your spirit guides even though the words are universal, in that they would apply to every reader, as well as you.

The Spiritual Realm

One of the most important points to always remember, embrace, and fully accept is that we are all part of God. What distinguishes humans from every other living thing on Earth is that within each of us is God's spirit—which, as I've explained, provides us with our immortality. Because this is inside of us, it gives us tremendous power, as well as accompanying responsibilities that humankind is not always able to properly handle. . . . Man gives life, man takes life. Man plants a tree, man cuts a tree down. Man breeds animals, man kills animals. Man is able to create, and unfortunately, man is also able to destroy. Only when we understand the responsibilities of being a part of God can life surely become "on earth as it is in heaven."

But what does it mean to have the spirit of God inside of you? When I was speaking through the memory of Paul while under hypnosis, Julia Ingram (the past-life-regression hypnotist) asked me how Jeshua described our relationship with God. This is how I answered, through the soul mind of Paul:

> *Jeshua says that even though we often refer to God as the Father, that God is both the Father and the Mother. And that God has no single gender. That God is a force, an entity of love and life—that all of us are a part of. Think of a body of water—like a lake. And that lake, for purposes of understanding, is an energy force of love and wisdom and knowledge. Each drop of that water, of that lake, is part of the whole. And then we take a jar and dip it into the lake, which was made up of thousands and thousands and thousands of little drops of water. These are part of the whole of that lake. We then scatter the drops in different places. Each little drop is put into the body of a newborn. Inside each of those people would be a part of the lake, even if they didn't recognize it. And that little portion of the lake is eternal, is everlasting. . . . It is what gives us life. When that little part of that lake leaves the body, the body no longer has life. Now if we equate that lake, instead, to being God, a different form of energy, rather than a lake, then we have a better understanding of why Jeshua says that we are part of God, just as that drop of water was once part of the lake. And if that drop of water were to return eventually to that lake, it would then be again at one with the rest of the lake. So it is when our spirit becomes at one again, not only in thought, but physically with God, that [we again are] one with God.*

I don't know how to describe God. I don't know if God is an entity that has human features, is an energy beyond description, or represents Him- or Herself as a brilliant light that is omniscient and omnipresent. I will not rely on what other authors have used as their descriptions of God, angels, or spirit guides, for I have committed to only rely on what I myself have witnessed and experienced. And that is what I shall share with you. I won't be quoting the thoughts or opinions of others, for I have no way of knowing whether their information is accurate, which indeed it may be, or the product of their imagination or an illusion. I'm only comfortable sharing with you what I've seen with my own eyes and what I've been personally told by Spirit.

I have, however, come to understand, believe, and accept that miracles do happen, for I have witnessed them and been the recipient of them many times. As I said in the Introduction, I define a miracle as being the intervention of God in our lives. But since I'm not able to define God, I've had to examine these miracles from a different perspective. And this has led me to believe that there is indeed a hierarchy in the spiritual world, as well as a collection of spiritual entities that influence our lives and are part of God's system.

I choose to think of God as the Chief Executive Officer of the corporation that has created both our world and the spiritual world, that manages the realm of Spirit and interacts with us on this Earthly plane. I think of the spiritual entities that collectively assist God as a part of Oneness. And *we* are also included within this enormous collaborating scheme—for we are the shareholders of the corporation; and God, the master guides, and the angels are the officers. So when I refer to Oneness, I am including everyone.

Unlike our forefathers of 2,000 years ago, I don't think of the spiritual world as being located above us in the sky, but rather functioning in a realm simultaneously with our material world, but at a totally different frequency. This dimension exists at a different vibration than ours does. And spiritual entities have the ability to function within our dimension, seeing us, hearing us, and involving themselves in our lives when they choose to, as they did when they woke up the Canadian businessman in Geneva. And as they did one night later, also rousing my friend Rick Eckert at 4:44 A.M. and having him write down their messages.

At times I can feel their presence when they choose to let me know they are with me. I'll feel a vibration, almost like a chill, that begins at the bottom of my back and runs up my spine until it reaches my shoulders. At times it's the sensation one has when one speaks of getting "goose bumps." I've never felt fear or apprehension when in their presence. Instead, I've felt appreciation, heartfelt warmth, and love.

In the final sections of this chapter, I'll be discussing our relationship with the cousins of our spirit guides, so to speak: our angels.

Seeing Angels

After *The Messengers* had become a bestseller, in every city where I went to give a presentation—whether it be New York; Washington, D.C.; Atlanta; Miami; Denver; or Los Angeles—there were always a few people in the audience who told me afterward that they had seen an angel or angels on the stage with me as I spoke. These people weren't sitting next to one another, nor were they in line together waiting for their book to be signed. No matter where I was, they always provided me with the exact same description of one angel in particular: it wore lavender, was about seven feet tall, and stood behind me to my right.

I can recall giving a presentation one night at the Unity Church in Naples, Florida, where more than 1,400 people had come to listen to my messages. I'd arrived in town three days earlier so that I could spend time with someone I'd come to love and admire: Ruth Montgomery, the world-famous spiritual author who had previously been a famous nationally syndicated columnist for major news publications, covering politics and political figures. Ruth sat in the first row, and I was honored to introduce her to the audience. But I will never forget one letter I received about a week later from someone who had also been there that night.

He wrote to me in very shaky handwriting, and it was obvious he was quite elderly. He tried to describe the spiritual energy he'd felt in that sanctuary that night, and he said it was beyond anything he'd ever experienced before. Then he wrote that he had witnessed something on the stage standing behind me that had literally taken his breath away. He had removed his glasses and wiped them with a handkerchief, for he couldn't believe his eyes. He said that tears began to roll down his cheeks, and although he was embarrassed to tell me about it, he proceeded to describe the seven-foot-tall angel in lavender.

I had always accepted these occurrences as part of my life . . . the cards that I'd been dealt, so to speak. But they—along with hundreds of other experiences I've had, some of which I'm sharing with you in this book—gave me an unwavering belief in God and the spiritual world. I was left with absolutely no doubt in my mind about the existence of a Divine order. I feel a sadness for those who do have doubts, for I know with all my heart and soul that if they had experienced the same events that I have in my life, there wouldn't be any atheists or agnostics, and we truly would live in a different world than we do. I'm hopeful that in these pages I can help nonbelievers and skeptics see the truth.

Prior to my personal experiences, I would have placed an angel in the same category as the Tooth Fairy and the Easter Bunny. But how do I deny what others have told me they've seen standing behind me on stages all across the country . . . people who don't know each other, each providing the same description of the seven-foot-tall angel in lavender?

Two angel mystics I know have both told me that angels are androgynous, although they look feminine. Also, unlike spirit guides, they've never lived on Earth as humans.

The word *angel* comes from the translation of an Aramaic word meaning "messenger." Among the five pages that my friend Rick had written that Sunday at 4:44 A.M., the angels guided him to draw a triangle and label the three points "Father," "Son," and the "Holy Ghost." Then they had Rick write: "Man has forgotten God's messengers," and draw a diamond with the same labels, but adding *angels* in the fourth corner.

On January 14, 1995, when I had my first angelic experience, I stated: "I am so blessed, for God is talking to me." And they corrected me, saying: "Not God—His guides."

I have come to believe that at different times angels will come into your life to protect you when you're in danger, inspire you when you're down, and assist you when you're in need. But if you're a couch potato, you most surely would have a couch-potato angel assigned to you—not that there is anything wrong with a couch potato or a couch-potato angel. Yet why would God waste a highly trained, energetic angel on a couch potato?

Angelic Intervention

I now know that there was a time when angelic intervention once saved my life, although it took me many years to realize it. I was in my late 20s and was helping my friend Bob Stearns pioneer a corporation where he was the director of marketing. We were traveling from Northern California, where we both lived at the time, to Salt Lake City, Utah, in the middle of winter. I was driving my four-door Ford LTD, and we had reached Donner Pass in the Sierra Nevada.

The sky was blue, the roads were clear, and I was going about 55 miles per hour. To my right was a drop of thousands of feet, and there was no guardrail. I was driving on the outside lane, the cliff side, of a four-lane road. We came to the peak of the mountain on our left, and it cast a huge shadow across the entire road. All of a sudden we hit sheer ice—the shadow had prevented it from being melted by the sun—and the car began to skid. It actually spun an exact 180 degrees. I found myself driving in the opposite direction, and the sheer mountain drop was now on my left.

Visualize what it would have looked like if you came upon us: a blue four-door sedan traveling almost 60 miles an hour, driving backward on ice, with a drop of thousands of feet down a mountainside only three or four feet from the car's tires.

We began to edge over to the side of the cliff, and then something happened that I cannot explain: the car began to spin again—not 181, not 179, but exactly *180* degrees. We were now traveling forward in the direction we had started. I waited until we came to a shoulder about a half mile farther on, and then I pulled over. I shut the engine off, and Bob and I looked at each other. We hadn't said a word during that entire experience. We reached out and shook hands, again in total silence, and then sat there for about five minutes.

What are the odds of the car spinning both times exactly 180 degrees? What are the odds that it wouldn't have spun just a little more and careened off the road, dropping thousands of feet down the mountainside? *What are the odds?* One out of a thousand? One out of ten thousand? I've relived that scene many times in my mind. I now have no doubt that Divine intervention took place on that mountaintop, or I wouldn't be writing this book and sharing this story with you today.

Thank you, angels. I owe you one.

In the next chapter we will continue our journey by exploring the subject I believe has the greatest effect on our lives. I am convinced that the most influential factors determining who we are, our likes and dislikes, the talents we have and those we lack . . . are our past-life experiences. Yes, we will be delving into the world of reincarnation.

Chapter 8

REINCARNATION

There are four elements commonly believed to influence who we are upon our birth. The two that are most accepted and understood within our society are: (1) our genes and DNA, and (2) the environment we grow up in. Some people put much stock in a third element, astrology—the position of the planets when we are born. If indeed we *are* affected by astrology, I don't think this element is very significant.

Countless individuals believe that our genes and DNA, which are inherited from our parents, play the most important role in our lives. Yet just as many believe that the environment we grow up in is the most influential factor with respect to who we are today and who we are to become.

But isn't it interesting that we can see children who are born in the same family (and therefore share virtually the same genetics); are raised in the same environment; and yet are tremendously different in their achievements, their talents, their intellect, and in many cases, their ability to distinguish right from wrong?

Imagine four children born in the same household: One becomes a college professor and scientist. Another grows up to become a professional musician, the only one in the family having musical talent. A third is committed to a religious life and enters the priesthood, and the fourth decides to lead a life of crime. How could this be, considering they came from the same environment and share most of the same genes?

The answer, I have been told by Spirit over and over, lies in the fourth element—*our past lives*—the effect of which is many times greater than the other three elements combined.

We enter this world with a soul that is the embodiment of all our experiences from our previous lifetimes. Even with twins, we can see at a very early age that one of them may be outgoing, the other shy. One child may be generous in sharing, while the other holds on to every toy for dear life. One learns very quickly, yet the other needs continual help. There is no greater influence on each and every one of us than our past-life experiences.

Homosexuality and Reincarnation

For years scientists and others who study human behavior have been trying to find an explanation for why some people have an attraction to those of the same gender. They have attempted to determine if homosexuality is the result of a gene that causes that sexual preference or some other factor. This issue has been debated by many, and none have found any evidence to support a definitive conclusion.

I have been told by Spirit that the explanation for homosexuality isn't complicated: the reason people are homosexual is that they've lived many of their past lives as someone of the opposite gender.

Take the example of a gay man. Let's assume he lived the past 20 lifetimes as a female and decided to experience his current life as a male. The decision to change genders may arise for karmic reasons, or to gain insights from the perspective of a different gender. But that person can't make the transition in one lifetime from all of the desires and personality traits of his past 20 lives as a female.

If the man in this lifetime was also very effeminate in his body language and preferred to wear feminine clothing, it might truly be his first incarnation as a male. On the other hand, if he were conventionally masculine in almost every way other than his preference for male companionship, or was perhaps bisexual, it could be his second or third male incarnation.

I feel confident that if a study was done using past-life hypnotic regression on a substantial number of gay males (who might also act very feminine) or gay females (who could act very masculine), it would confirm that they had been the opposite gender in their past lives.

The Celebrity Phenomenon

Perhaps you're having difficulty accepting the possibility of reincarnation; or maybe you're a firm believer, but you simply doubt my claim of having experienced an incarnation as a biblical figure, the Apostle Paul. You may be asking the question: *Why are people always convinced they were famous in a past life, like Cleopatra or Napoléon?*

I can recall being interviewed by three hosts on a noon TV show in New York City. One of them was a man who wasn't the regular host but was a substitute that day. He undoubtedly wanted to impress the thousands of people watching the show, and the first words out of his mouth were: "How come you people who believe in reincarnation all think you were somebody famous in your past life?" I had to spend a very valuable chunk of my 15-minute segment to explain to him that this isn't true.

Statistics show that perhaps one out of many, many thousands under hypnosis identify with someone who may have been famous. The others lived normal lives: typical fathers and mothers, husband and wives . . . people trying to meet the challenges of everyday life, raising children and keeping a home. After discounting the pretenders—those who knowingly pass themselves off as having been a celebrity—it is indeed a very rare occasion to encounter someone who was a notable person in a past life. But as a hypnotist once said to me years ago, famous people get reborn again just like everybody else.

If you don't believe that I did indeed have a past life as the Apostle Paul, I totally understand and am sympathetic to that. I happened to reject this idea myself for many years. I had tremendous difficulty accepting it, and then once the proof was overwhelming, I was still reluctant to make such a declaration. But I now know with 100 percent certainty that 2,000 years ago my spirit and soul did live as Paul. I could fill a book just recounting the incidents, evidence, and verifications that finally convinced me to accept what I know now to be the truth.

What finally made me move forward was an appointment I had with a well-known psychic, Laurie McQuary, who lived in my city. Laurie was particularly famous in Japan, where she would help the authorities find missing people.

My session with her began by her asking me if my right knee still hurt. And it did, for I'd been running about six or seven miles a day up and down hills. A little later she told me that I was dating a woman whose parents objected to the relationship. My girlfriend (now my wife) was Catholic and I wasn't, and I had been divorced. Laurie told me both parents would end up in the hospital the next year, and one would pass away there. (Indeed, the following year both were hospitalized, and my wife's mother did pass away while a patient.)

In the middle of the consultation, Laurie stood up, her eyes wide as saucers, and said, "Oh my God. You knew Jesus." She followed that up by admonishing me for not moving ahead with the purpose in my life. The next day she and I had lunch together, and she told me of a woman she knew who was an expert at doing past-life-regression hypnosis. I agreed that the three of us should meet, which we did shortly thereafter.

Thus it came about that Julia Ingram and I spent the next six months capturing on tape many hours of my regressions to 2,000 years ago. And this was how I was finally placed on the path that I'm on today.

A Dream . . . or a Past Life?

I want to share a personal story with you that I've only told perhaps three or four people in my life. It began when I was 11 years old, when I had a very unusual dream. In it, I was a young man in my early 20s, and I was from Paris. What's amazing is that the dream took place entirely in French, although neither I nor any member of my family spoke a word of the language. In fact, I didn't know *anybody* who did. And the main person in my dream—me—was a grown man. How could this be?

In my dream I graduated from the Sorbonne in Paris, which would be the equivalent to Harvard University in the U.S. Upon graduating, I was drafted into the French army, as the time period was the First World War. I saw myself with a large number of other soldiers aboard a troop train. We were all in uniform and carried our rifles with us at our seats. The floor of the car was exposed, raw wood, as were the walls and ceilings. The builders had obviously intentionally left off finishing the train using normal materials.

The next scene found me up against a well. I was somewhere in Belgium. A rotary had been formed around the well, and across the street from me was a four-story apartment building. I was shooting my rifle at German soldiers on the third floor, who were returning my fire.

All of a sudden my vision rose up, and my "sight" was hovering about 20 feet above my discarded body, which had been shot in the chest and was slumped against the well. I felt no pain or emotional stress, for my spirit left my body instantaneously.

I don't remember being upset upon waking, or any of the emotions I had at that time. But I do remember being tremendously puzzled: How could I have had a dream totally in French when I wasn't able to speak it? How could I have been a different person than Nick Bunick, and how could I have *died* in my dream? It didn't make any sense. I was trying to comprehend what I'd experienced through the mind of an 11-year-old boy. And I didn't ask my parents or any friends for advice, since I knew that they wouldn't have been able to process this experience.

Years later when I was in my 40s, a friend of mine named Cheri called from Sun Valley, Idaho. Her husband, Tom Drougas, had become a professional football player after graduating from a college in the state where I lived, and they were now living in Sun Valley and working in real estate. The three of us shared common spiritual beliefs, so Cheri wanted to tell me about the psychic reading she'd had the night before.

Cheri asked the psychic if she and I had known each other in a past life, for she told me she'd always had a feeling that we had. He responded by telling her that she and I had been good friends in Paris in the early 1900s and that I'd been killed as a soldier fighting the Germans in Belgium. I had never told *anybody* that story before.

Not too long after that, my parents came out from Massachusetts to visit me. While my mother and I were walking along the beach, I asked her if I'd ever mentioned anything about France when I was a child.

She began to laugh and told me that when I was about seven or eight, I used to insist that if anyone asked her where she was originally from, she wasn't to tell them Russia, but instead say that she was from France. She also told me that as a child I would collect every magazine photo I could find of Parisian scenes: the Arc de Triomphe, the Seine River, and the Champs-Élysées, with its cobblestone streets and outdoor restaurants. I hadn't remembered doing any of the things my mother mentioned, but it certainly fit in with my dream.

Years later I went on my first vacation to France with my wife. I will never forget the feeling that took hold as soon as we arrived, as if I had returned home after being away many years. I was able to walk the streets of Paris as if I knew where I was going—to the shopping district, to the Eiffel Tower, to the Sorbonne—but I had my greatest experience in a church in Les Invalides.

After we walked across the famous bridge over the Seine, there was a sidewalk through the park that separated it into two halves. On one side elderly men were playing games like horseshoes and boccie ball, and the other was filled with children throwing Frisbees and participating in other kids' games. The sidewalk ended where two buildings sat back-to-back. We visited the second building first: a museum encompassing the ornate tombs of Napoléon and his family. But the first building, a church, caused me to have the most incredible sense of déjà vu.

Inside, flags were hung from the ceiling of the old and ornate structure, representing all the different countries that had occupied France during its history. There were only three people in the entire place besides my wife and me . . . and then it happened:

I experienced the church so full of people that there wasn't an empty seat. Everyone was singing in French in low voices. I could see, hear, and smell these people; and I could almost reach out and touch them.

Tears began running down my cheeks, and my eyes were half-closed. When my wife asked, "Nick, what's the matter?" I put my finger to my lips and said, "Shhh." I was in "real" time, but a hundred years ago, when I was a student at the Sorbonne and would visit this church.

Years later I allowed myself to be hypnotized and regressed, and I asked the hypnotist to take me back to that same lifetime in France I had experienced in my childhood dream. Under hypnosis, I'd again graduated from the Sorbonne, but this time I was attending a going-away party in a tavern with some friends. I don't remember that scene being in my dream, although it may have been, since I wouldn't have necessarily remembered everything. I also experienced the troop train and my death scene against the well in Belgium.

This was one of several past lifetimes I'd accessed, but this one was so convincing because of the dream, my Sun Valley friend's psychic reading, my mother's recollection of me tearing out pictures of Paris scenes when I was a child, and my incredible experience in that church. Considering the above events, can you think of any explanation other than that I lived my last lifetime in France?

Chapter 9

JOURNEY OF LIFE

I used to be concerned that someday when we all eventually become part of Oneness, we'll lose our individuality. This really bothered me until I was finally provided with a valid explanation by Spirit:

If you were to listen to an orchestra, you'd be hearing the collective sound from a group of individuals. You might conclude, based on your own criteria and personal taste, whether or not the music was enjoyable, the group was talented, and the experience was entertaining. You would be forming an opinion on the totality of sounds being expressed.

But within that group, each individual musician makes his or her own personal and unique contribution. Some may be talented, and others may not be. Some may be great performers, while a few may be limited in their skills. The blending together of the skills of these individuals produces a collective sound you may find positive or negative, but is that not true of everything in life? A sports team may have individual stars who can put up great numbers, along with others who are just mediocre. But if the stars dominate, the team will succeed. If the stars can't compensate for the inferior skills of their teammates, they'll be defeated.

Collectiveness

In every facet of life, we're exposed to the collective attributes of the individuals who are part of a group—the collective intellects of those who make the decisions within our government, for instance, or the collective hate of those who are committed to bringing harm to us.

If the majority of political leaders are filled with hatred and are motivated by greed and the need for power at the expense of others, and if they're capable of motivating the majority of those under their leadership to share those feelings with them and support their efforts, that society would be looked upon as "evil." And yet there may be individuals within it who are loving and compassionate and aren't in agreement with the leaders and their followers. But the voices of this minority will go unheard, their good intentions getting lost among the collective forces of evil emanating from the majority. If their dissent is too vocal or too conspicuous, they may even be imprisoned or put to death.

This is not to be confused with the Oneness I speak of in the spiritual world. The phenomenon I'm describing is what takes place in our dimension, in our world, when the collective consciousness and will of the majority has its way. It was collective evil consciousness that created Nazi Germany, as well as the ruthless Bolshevik regime in the early 20th century in Russia. It was collective evil consciousness that gave birth to the Crusades, which killed many thousands of innocent people. It also created the Holocaust, which took the lives of millions . . . along with the turmoil and pain throughout the world today caused by groups of people who are motivated by hate rather than love, who are perpetrators of evil rather than good.

God's Gifts

There are some who cry out in anguish, "Where is God? Why doesn't God intervene and stop the suffering of young children in Africa, prevent the fighting among Protestants and Catholics in

Ireland, and put an end to the turmoil and hostilities in the Holy Land? Has God forsaken us and forgotten His children?"

For those of us who believe in a Divine power, we understand that we are the children of God. We understand that God created our "playground," the world we live in. And God created an environment for us to play in that varies with the seasons and that gives us night and day; food for us to grow, harvest, and eat; and the elements that yield potential pleasure alongside pain, our comfort as well as our discomfort.

And it's logical, then, that God would have said to us: "It is now your world and your lives. I have given you the free will to play the game as you choose. Hopefully to love each other rather than hate each other, to create rather than destroy, to share rather than be selfish . . . to have compassion rather than be indifferent to the suffering of your brothers and sisters. I have given you the intellect to reason, the physical ability to help others, the resources to create and sustain life."

But God also gave us the greatest gift He could possibly bestow upon us: His energy and spirit, which resides in every one of us. We are children of God. We are each a part of the Oneness that we know as God, just as the musician is part of the orchestra, to the player is part of the team, the politician is part of the government, and the individual citizen is part of society.

Your Contribution

You tend to make a contribution to your family unit and the group of people you refer to as your friends, the company you work for (if you're employed), and the country of your citizenship—but you can also contribute on the greatest scale of all: to the society of humanity of which you are a part.

What will be your contribution to that collective consciousness, that collective energy? Will you contribute fear or love, selfishness or compassion, hope or despair? If you first look at the smallest group you're a part of and commit to being a positive influence within that unit—to inspiring others to share the common goal of manifesting love and compassion—you can assure your positive contribution and impact. And that group, in turn, can affect a larger segment of the society it functions within. And this continues to expand to have an influence on your state, your country, and the world.

Your awakening begins when you discover your own identity. You are part of the divinity. You are part of Oneness. You are part of God. The spirit of God resides within you.

You must not separate yourself from God. If you do, you will experience confusion, disharmony, strife, torment, and spiritual starvation. By recognizing that you are part of God and are manifesting His love through you, you will experience the greatest joy of life, which has nothing to do with wealth, power, or material things. There is nothing *wrong* with wealth, power, and material things—but, as Spirit told me, they are like the rain that cannot distinguish need, which falls on the ocean as well as in the valley.

True happiness—the type that encompasses your soul, heart, mind, and spirit—comes from recognizing that you are a child of God, that you are *part* of God. This is accomplished when you manifest God's will by sharing your love and compassion for His children, your fellow human beings, who are all your brothers and sisters.

Relight the lantern that is within your being. Rekindle the flame and feel the warmth that flows from the Divine spirit within you. Live now in recognition of who you are, and manifest yourself as part of God, which is the true essence of your being. That is who you *really* are.

Until you recognize your identity and live accordingly, you are doing an injustice to yourself. You are denying your immortality, as well as your ability to enjoy life and let others enjoy life *through* you. Accept it, cherish it, and use it at every moment, for it is a gift that God has given to you.

The Journey

You are on a journey. You've been on it since the day you entered into this lifetime. The destination was predetermined: it is your destiny to become at one with God, not just a part of God, but to become *at one with* Him. When you do so, you are like the individual musician who is part of the orchestra, the player who is part of the team. You don't lose your individuality, but what an indescribable joy, to become at one with God!

Every experience you have was created by your actions and decisions. Yet there is no one journey that is preferable to another. God doesn't care if you must be taught the same lesson a hundred times. It's your choice, and no two journeys are alike.

There are always events occurring in your life. It's as if you're watching a play in which you're viewing yourself and all the hardships and challenges that you're exposed to. Don't you see that you created them in order to allow yourself to develop greater understanding and awareness?

You created every event in your own world, for you are the playwright and the star of your play. It is through your disappointments and heartaches that you experience the most personal growth. Your greatest lessons are learned from your most painful moments, trials, and tribulations.

Don't look upon those past experiences as though you've been a victim and ask, "Why me, God?" Instead, look upon them as an opportunity to grow, to enhance your understanding that you are a part of God, a child of God . . . that you are capable of showing strength rather than weakness, humility rather than anger . . . that you can manifest God's love to others, rather than resentment and bitterness.

What an incredible journey you have created for yourself. You may have chosen to move away from the community you grew up in. Perhaps you've opted to travel to many different locations, stopping at some that you then called home. You made hundreds of friends along the way. You developed a variety of skills, different ways to apply yourself to earn an income. You may have brought children into the world, whom you share with God—you're their parent, but God is as well. What an incredible experience it is to share parenthood with God, if you've made that decision!

If you've experienced the pain of losing a child or a loved one, take comfort in knowing that this individual is with the Creator, Who will see that he or she never experiences discomfort or hardship while in Divine guardianship in the other dimension. God lent you His child, and He will take care of your loved one until you are with him or her again.

Climbing the Stairs

During the journey of life you are on, your goal—your destiny—is to become at one with God and achieve Christ Consciousness. Visualize that pyramid of a thousand steps that I spoke of in the Introduction to Part II. At the top is God, and during your lifetimes you are ascending the stairs so that you may reach it. You may ascend one step in a week or a month. Sometimes you might have an experience in which you manifested God's love with such great passion—touched someone's life in such an incredibly positive, wonderful way—that within a single day you leaped up five or ten steps, each taking you closer to being at one with God.

Every person is at a different level on the stairway to God. You may be on the 111th step . . . or the 320th, 444th, or 700th. You can look at the lives of loved ones, friends, or neighbors and possibly determine with fairly good accuracy which step they are on in their journey to becoming at one with God and achieving Christ Consciousness. But don't judge others based on where you consider them to be. All people must make the journey at their own pace. You mustn't feel you're better than another because you think you're at a higher level, for that may cause you to fall back several steps, since this is a reflection of ego and isn't consistent with the part of you that is God.

Nor should you feel inferior to another whom you recognize to be on a higher level of the stairway than you. You are not "less than." Your destiny is the same—becoming at one with God—and you will achieve it within your own time frame. But you will be rewarded as you help others fulfill *their* destiny, for in doing so, you're manifesting God's will and His love.

And may God bless you as you continue on your journey.

The Poem

In this chapter, I've made many references to the journey you're on. This brought to my mind a poem my spirit guides created a few years ago on that subject. Just like the poem in Chapter 3, one day I found it undated in a folder in one of my filing cabinets. I have no recollection of having written it—although I know I did so, for it was in my handwriting—but again, please understand that I do not *write* poetry. The words are not mine, but rather, are created by Spirit. And there's so much truth to them, as we are taken from childhood to the later years in our lives. . . .

Journey of Life

Our journey began many years ago,
We traveled a great distance from the start.
We climbed over mountains, through valleys and fields,
At times we would have quit, had we a fainter heart.

It began with our young faces shining and bright,
Teachers, working hard among our class.
Books and pencils and papers were our tools,
Great efforts were made toward each lad and lass.

The seasons came fast and sometimes slow,
There were moments that were sad and moments of fun.
Winter brought cold and mounds of snow,
But it was always followed by warmth and sun.

Friends were made we knew for life,
Companions we would never forget.
Our lives were full of so much joy,
To our young world, we had little debt.

Then it was time to move along,
To compete, we must educate.
And the clock of life did not stand still,
Step by step, we rose to graduate.

New faces, new names, more demands were made,
And hours of study grew longer.
New foods, new clothes, new songs were played,
And our bodies grew older and stronger.

We cheered for our colors and sang foolish songs
And thought that ours was the best.
We worked so hard to become so smart,
To distinguish ourselves from the rest.

The important day came, no longer a youth,
We dressed alike in robes of black.
They told us we were now adults,
Full speed ahead, no time to look back.

We scrambled around, new towns and streets,
We knocked on doors to find our place.
It was a new beginning, one more time,
And we were caught in the middle of the race.

Two or three times we changed jobs
Till we found what we knew was right.
Now our energies could be devoted
To reaching our furthest height.

We sought a friend and chose our mate,
We created home and the young ones came.
We couldn't understand where the dollar went
As we strove for our fortune and fame.

We clawed and pulled and pushed and shoved,
Was not life's object to "get ahead"?
Nothing was of more importance,
What other path was there to tread?

The home grew larger, the closets fuller,
The lawns were green, the cars were sleek.

The prizes were great, accounts were bigger,
We could not have done it, had we been meek.

But one day did arrive not too long ago
When the mirror showed us truth.
The years had gone by so fast,
What happened to our youth?

The old friends we had made for life,
We could not remember their names.
The silly songs, the parties, and heroes we cheered,
We couldn't even remember the games.

We think of thoughts not thought before
And the purpose of the race we ran.
Of the mountain we hiked and climbed
And of the ocean that we swam.

We ask questions of ourselves we had never asked before,
We wonder if it is too late.
We had followed the same path as the others,
But should some other road have been our fate?

Learning and knowledge did not make us smart,
Our slower step finally made us look back.
Was the prize really worth the running?
Or had we raced on the wrong track?

But as long as our spirit on this journey does travel,
We can still choose to finish it right.
For it is more important to climb the right mountain,
For at the top is a spectacular sight.

We should not care how many years it will take,
For the path is covered with warmth and love.
We should not care if time allows us to reach the top
As long as we continue to climb above.

For joy and bliss is for everybody:
The rich and the poor, the young and the old.
Let us not tarry any longer, come join us
If you are also racing on the wrong road.

I loved the analogies that Spirit provided: climbing mountains and swimming in oceans, representing the challenges in our lives; and the changing of the seasons, representing the years going by as we're reaching young adulthood and then the transition from grade school to higher levels of education.

When we finally graduate, an entirely new set of challenges lies before us: looking for our true vocation, getting married, accumulating things in life we feel are important to us. But then the question is raised: did we neglect the most important part of all, which is our spiritual side—our relationship with God and the purpose of our lives?

These are the same two issues that I discussed earlier in the book. I suggest you read Spirit's poem again and look for the nuances provided as you took the journey of life.

It often seems as if the journey we undergo in our lifetime has been predetermined. Does our free will allow us to make our own decisions, or have our lives been programmed to follow a pathway that has already been agreed upon? The next chapter will deal with this complicated issue in great depth.

Chapter 10

Predetermination

I've often heard people ask whether our lives are predetermined. There *is* an answer, but it's not a simple one. The challenge for me is to word it in such a manner that it's understandable.

Sometimes as an author you can sit in front of your computer, and the words come out faster than you're capable of typing. Other times you can sit there staring at the keyboard for many, many minutes, trying to figure out how to put the thoughts running through your mind into words . . . which is what I'm experiencing right now. So are you ready? Here goes.

To truly understand the answer to the question of whether our lives are predestined, you must realize that in our mortal world, we live in a dimension governed by linear time; this is experienced and measured in frames that we identify as seconds, minutes, hours, days, weeks, months, years, and so on. We must live today before we can experience tomorrow. That is how our dimension functions.

But what if we lived in a dimension in which we experienced in a day what is the equivalent of a year of a person's life in *this* dimension? For example, every emotion and every event that occurred over the course of a year—the pleasure and the pain, the successes and the failures—would all transpire within a day. I'm sure you're asking how that could be possible. How can you condense into one day the experiences of one year?

You might better relate to this by envisioning the experiences of one year happening instead over a *two*-year period. Under that scenario, time moves more slowly, with the events that took place in 12 months stretched over the course of 24. Perhaps this makes it easier to understand the concept that the linear time we experience in this dimension could conceivably be a different length in another dimension—or if you prefer, in another state of being.

Now let's look at one more example illustrating the possible differences between time, space, and events. Let's assume that you live three miles from a favorite place you like to frequent on a regular basis. One day you decide to get to this location by walking, enjoying the scenery and the view, and it takes you one hour to get there. The next day you take the same trip, follow the same route, and pass the same scenery—but this time you travel by bike, and it takes you 20 minutes to get to your destination. And the next day you again take the trip, by car this time, and the duration of the journey is only six minutes. Same journey, same scenes, same distance . . . yet all three experiences took place within a different time frame.

Having exercised your own intellectual understanding of the concept of dimensional time, let's now answer the question: *Are our lives predetermined?*

No, our lives are *not* predetermined. "Predetermined" means that events would happen to you regardless of your choices or your free will. But *you* are the producer of your own movie. You write your own "script" detailing what you will experience, one event at a time, one choice at a time, one success or failure at a time . . . each moment of joy and each moment of sadness. But there are times when you are the victim of events you have no conscious control over, such as being in an accident or losing a loved one. The same is also true of positive events—for example, great opportunities offered to you that you didn't anticipate and perhaps felt that you may not have earned.

These possibilities—some that you could expect to occur and some that come as total surprises—are not predetermined, yet *all* of them have already happened to you in a different time dimension. In reality, your entire life has already taken place, from your birth to the transition of your soul. But you are now experiencing these events in this lifetime based on linear time within *our* dimension, unfolding for you on a day-to-day basis.

Life as a Movie

Let me provide you with an analogy that will hopefully help make this concept more clear to you.

Let's assume you haven't yet seen *Titanic* and plan to go to the theater tomorrow evening. You know that the movie has already been made—there is a beginning and an end, both of which have already been captured on film. You just haven't seen it yet, even though it does exist as a finished product. Now you're going to go to the theater tomorrow, and you'll sit there for three hours and experience the movie from start to finish. But you recognize that the script has already been written, the actors have already played their roles, and you are viewing something that has already transpired.

The same is true of your life. Outside of the linear time of this dimension, your entire life has already taken place, but you're now living these events on a day-by-day basis. If you're destined to live in your present body for 100 years before your soul makes its transition and you're now 50, in reality you have viewed 50 percent of the movie of your life. Every year you are catching up with an additional one percent of your future.

If you grasp this concept, then you understand how legitimate psychics or seers can tell you of your past or future. By some metaphysical gift, they have the ability to connect with your soul mind. They're able to play your video in reverse as well as fast-forward, and are able, in a matter of minutes, to retrieve information regarding what has happened to you and what events are to come. It would be the same as if you were sitting at home with a

DVD of *Titanic* playing on your TV and using a remote to go back to an earlier scene or to see what occurs later on, rather than viewing it one frame at a time.

So our lives are not predetermined. You have the absolute gift of free will that God has given to you. You write your own script. You're not only the screenwriter; you are also the producer, director, and star of the story of your life.

Every decision that you're going to make, you have *already* made. You'll just have to wait until it's time for you to *see* what choices are required of you, and since you have the experience of making them on a day-to-day basis, you're catching up with your future.

That was how psychic Laurie McQuary was able to tell me during my reading that my future wife's mother and father would both be in the hospital, and one of them would pass away. That was how psychic Duane Berry was able to tell me that there would come a time when I would be speaking in front of thousands of people in live audiences, and millions on television . . . and 20 years later I *was* speaking in front of those audiences—and will be again in the future. How else could they have known, if they weren't able to see that those future events had in reality already happened?

But can you make a decision that will alter future events? Yes, absolutely, and you have already done so. Without yet knowing it in this dimension, you have already made every decision in your life you have to make. This includes the ones you'll experience in the future that you thought would transpire in a different way. You'll just have to wait until it's time for you to see what decisions you have to make, and then have the experience of making them in the present.

Sharing Truth

I wrote the previous section yesterday afternoon. Last night, as I thought about what I shared with you, I began to worry that it might be too much. That it might be too esoteric. That you might feel that the concept was just not believable, or misunderstand what I was trying to say because of my own limited writing skills. So earlier today I decided to delete this entire chapter, for as I've said, my credibility with you is of the utmost importance to me.

Late this morning I had an appointment with Laurie, who I believe is one of the most gifted psychics in the world. Over lunch I told her what I'd written in this chapter and my resolution to delete it, and why.

She responded, "But what you described is exactly correct. That is the way it is. You *cannot* delete it. It doesn't make a difference if everybody doesn't understand it or accept it. It *is* the truth. And didn't you say the title of your book is *Time for Truth?* If you delete it, then maybe you should change your title to *It Is Not Yet Time for Truth."*

Laurie encouraged me to make sure I explain this important question of predetermination properly. Allow me to do so one more time, in summary fashion:

No, your life is not predetermined. You have free will, a gift from God, which allows you to make your own decisions. And you will make thousands between now and the end of your life. In a different dimension, as I described in the early part of this chapter, you have experienced your entire life, but not in linear time as we know it in this mortal world. Your soul mind has knowledge of everything, although your conscious mind does not. Your conscious mind is discovering it, minute by minute, day by day, as you experience the entire lifetime that has been recorded in your soul mind.

That's how a psychic like Laurie can tell you what's going to happen in the future, as well as what has happened in your past. She has the ability to tap into your soul mind, and as if she had a remote, she can fast-forward into your future, as well as rewind into your past. In essence, that is how *I* am able to access those memories of the Apostle Paul . . . by tapping into my own soul mind.

Laurie doesn't wear a turban, nor does she own a crystal ball. She is an attractive woman with a professional-looking demeanor.

Laurie wasn't psychic as a child. At the age of 18, she had a horseback-riding accident on a bridge near Escondido, California, and remained in a coma for three weeks. After coming out of it, she found that her life had changed dramatically, as she discovered that she had the ability to access information through *extrasensory* perception—that is, beyond the normal five senses.

Laurie has now been practicing her profession for 25 years and is one of the most gifted psychics I've ever known. She gives approximately 120 readings a month and has been featured on the TV show *Psychic Detectives* several times, *Larry King Live* twice, and many other programs. She has also appeared on Japanese television. (You can visit her Website at: **www.lauriemcquary.com**.)

Laurie reminded me to emphasize the incredible importance that reincarnation plays in your life. You are tremendously influenced by your past lives, your positive karma as well as your negative karma. Reincarnation has influenced your value system, your degree of patience, your generosity, your fears, your talents, your interests, and hundreds of other aspects of your life that you have brought with you from your past lives. It's reincarnation that allows you to continue to climb the stairs of the pyramid, no matter how many lifetimes it takes, until you become at one with God and Christ Consciousness.

Having said all that, I urge you to never lose sight of the fact that you are not a human being who by coincidence has an eternal spirit and soul. As I have shared with you previously, you are a spirit with a soul who is having a human experience. You are an immortal child of God. The spirit of God resides within you and everyone. As Jeshua said 2,000 years ago, "Ye are gods."

Free Will

In reality, all of us are on the same journey, trying to fulfill the same destiny: to become at one with God, once we are able to reach the top stair of that pyramid. As we continue on our journey, it is impacted by the way we lead our lives and the degree to which it is consistent with the natural laws of the universe that God has created.

To some people, the journey is one of beauty. The weather is calm, the sky is pale blue, and they travel along feeling great joy. Others constantly find themselves in storms, in chaos and confusion. The weather is foul, which fills them with anger, hostility, and sadness.

What causes one person to live a life consistent with the natural laws of God and another to be in violation of those laws? As I shared with you earlier, it has to do with free will, which separates us from every other living thing on this planet. Free will is a gift that God gave to each and every one of us.

It's free will that allows us to progress in this lifetime and find happiness by being in accord with God's influence. It is our free will, bestowed by the Creator, that enables us to experience the joy of living by giving universal love to others and expressing universal compassion.

On the other hand, free will has inspired some individuals to live outside of the influence of God and not practice the natural laws of the universe. There is no external force compelling people to commit criminal acts or to exhibit evil or sinister behavior. There are no evil spirits or fictitious devils vying for our souls and minds. Rather, there are only the deliberate acts of individuals who, by virtue of free will, choose to put their wants above those of others, and in so doing, find themselves in disharmony with their own spirituality—that part of God that is inside them.

We're the only species alive able to distinguish right from wrong, morality from immorality. The natural laws of the universe are basic, and when we practice them, we're in harmony with our spiritual selves. When people are violating these laws by not embracing universal love and compassion, they do so deliberately and with free will. They then commit acts of aggression against others, exhibit a lack of empathy, and seek personal gratification at the expense of others.

The testing ground is this material world we now live in. Do we use our free will to practice that which gives happiness to others, or to seek personal gain at their expense? This is what distinguishes whether a person is moving up or down the stairway of the pyramid, and this is what causes one journey to be filled with joy and happiness and another to be characterized by anguish and emotional pain.

Nevertheless, we are on the *same* journey, even though its quality will differ greatly between those who are in harmony with God, and those who are not.

As I said, the earth is our testing ground. It is only here, in the material world, that we can advance toward our enlightenment, in our desire to experience the greatest treasures awaiting us someday when we become at one with God and Christ Consciousness. Only in the material world can we ascend the steps of the pyramid.

In school we're taught lessons, and if these are learned, we then advance to the next grade the following year. We're also given a vacation in between those school years. This isn't dissimilar to our spiritual growth: We have our lessons to learn in each lifetime. We then experience a spiritual "life" before we proceed to our next mortal lifetime. The level at which we enter into the spiritual world depends on how we lived our last life in the physical world—which step we were on when we made our transition.

If you lived your life as a bigot, full of hate and prejudice—whether it be for racial or religious reasons—it's very likely that you'll experience that same bigotry and hatred directed toward *you* in a future lifetime. It's not unlikely that the next time you're incarnated, you may be born into the very race or religion that your bigotry was directed toward so that you may feel the same pain and anguish you once inflicted on others. Or instead, you may live that next lifetime as a leader committed to challenging those prejudices.

It is through those type of experiences that we're able to learn, and become closer to reaching the spiritual perfection that we are all trying to attain. This, of course, is called karma.

Universal Love and Compassion

By the same token, once we learn to totally embrace universal love, compassion, and truth, so shall we receive the same. Acts of kindness and sensitivity to others are like the planting of seeds in a beautiful garden. For surely if the flowers don't bloom in this lifetime, they shall do so in another, to reward us for work we have done that is deserving of recognition.

It's crucial that you recognize and understand the natural laws of the universe. There is nothing more important in the world than that you extend universal love and compassion to others. Love has no anger, no pain, and no burdens to bear. It is pure and good and is the elixir to heal all problems. Our spiritual guides, our guardian angels, and Oneness all teach that love is the greatest power on Earth. Think how different our world would be if every human being lived his or her life filled with compassion for others and universal love. If all beings did so, there would be no weapons of mass destruction or wars; there would be no hunger. All efforts would be made to help others attain happiness and joy.

And love has no boundaries. It is one of the most contagious elements in the world. Express this feeling through your behavior, your body language, and the words you use to communicate with others and you'll find that you will receive the same in return. It's such an easy task and goal. It's also simple to test the results, whether you try it in the very simplest form by smiling at a stranger on the street and saying "Good morning," or by showing kindness to a clerk in a grocery store or a waitress in a restaurant.

Even though you may not know these individuals personally, simply show them acts of love, genuinely from the heart, by the look in your eyes, the smile on your face, and the words you choose. Then feel the joy of their responses and the love they give you in return once they understand that you're sincere.

To those who are closer to you, the love can be expressed with greater intimacy, whether it be a hug, a kiss, a gentle touch, or tender words. As Spirit once wrote to me: *"Be love and gentleness . . . and all around you, you shall create the same."* It's simple to live within God's natural laws of the universe, if you so choose.

Happiness is the quest of the majority of the people on Earth. But so many have been raised to believe that it is directly related to the acquisition of material wants. For the wealthy, it's judged by their peers in terms of the value of the homes they own, the private clubs they belong to, the clothes they wear, and the restaurants where they dine.

But in truth, happiness and joy are found in the relationships we have with others . . . by the compassion we show to them . . . and how we are perceived by those we care for.

There's No Such Thing as Death

There was a time when I feared death. I used to think, *How sad it is that someday I will no longer enjoy the things in life that bring me great joy and happiness.* I carried a heavy burden in my heart whenever I let myself consider that someday I would cease to be alive within this body. I felt that all my memories and all my thoughts—and yes, even all my achievements—mattered not, for I would no longer exist to be able to enjoy them, cherish them, and continue to remember them. But that is not the case, for our minds and our spirits are perpetual.

As your own transition approaches, may you have the wisdom, courage, and understanding to know that you shall soon be in pure spirit. And while you may no longer be embodied within your physical shell, you'll still have all the memories you've created in this lifetime. You'll have sympathy for those you leave behind who mourn you, and you'll have the spiritual wisdom to understand your relationship with God as well.

You'll understand that there is no such thing as death, but only the transition of the soul. You will surely miss the companionship of your loved ones when you're separated, but you may take solace and comfort in knowing that they still exist and you'll be with them in the future.

As your loved ones leave you in making their own transitions—whether they are young or old—it's important to understand that they are not in anguish or pain. Your loved ones in spirit are in God's light. They're experiencing joy, happiness, and serenity; and are basking in the universal consciousness of God's love. While they appreciate the feelings you have for them, emanating from what you consider your "loss," they don't want you to feel despair, hurt, or grief.

If they were able to talk directly to you, they would tell you that they aren't experiencing pain, sadness, or anxiety; rather, they're immersed in ecstasy and bliss. They would tell you that they're grateful for your love; and they want you to honor their memories, cherish your fond remembrances, and know that they are still with you. They want you to live your life to the fullest. That is their wish, and that is the most precious way in which you can show your love for them.

At times you will feel your loved ones' presence. They may come to you in your dreams and during meditation. They know that they are in your thoughts and prayers. But the most important thing for you to know is that your loved ones want you to enjoy life. The greatest gift you can give them is to continue loving them, allowing your love for them to be an inspiration to you. And through that love, to enjoy life every moment and let others enjoy life through you.

As we go through our lifetimes, we accumulate a substantial amount of negative karma when we don't practice universal love and compassion. This in turn leaves marks on our souls and can oftentimes lead to sickness, both physical and emotional. In the next chapter, we'll carry out a spiritual healing to release that negative karma.

Chapter 11

Forgiveness

As I've mentioned, after *The Messengers* was published, I conducted symposiums in major cities across the country. I always concluded the presentations by guiding those in the audience to participate in a spiritual healing. I've witnessed the joy that comes from opening the hearts and souls of many thousands of people as I applied the same techniques that Jeshua did thousands of years ago, which he also taught Paul.

It's through these spiritual healings that people have the opportunity to release negative karma by sincerely asking for and accepting forgiveness. This is karma accumulated as a result of previous actions, behavior that would not have been consistent with universal love and compassion. This negative karma sits heavily on the soul and can often produce emotional and physical stress and sickness. As I've watched these spiritual healings taking place, I've often felt as if I were in a time machine going back 2,000 years. I now ask you to join me in your own spiritual healing.

This type of healing can make a major difference in your life. It is one that can be continual, if you choose it to be. If you are willing, you should read this chapter once a week for the next four weeks so that it becomes a part of you, and so your soul can be cleansed and healed. The result will be that you will become closer to being at one with God.

Please select a quiet, peaceful place to read this chapter, either in your home or outdoors. Shut off all outside distractions so that you may join me in a focused meditation. Concentrate on the words that have been given to me that I now share with you. . . .

I ask that you totally relax, not only quieting your body, but also your heart and mind. Let your mind open the gateway to your soul. Allow your thoughts to be confined to what I am sharing with you, and do not permit any outside distractions to interfere with what we are now going to experience together.

I am asking that you first pray to God and ask His permission to participate in this spiritual healing. I suggest that you take 60 seconds or more and ask God, Jeshua, and your loving angels and guides for permission to be the recipient of this spiritual healing. Ask that they also help you to open your heart and soul to these words. Please do so now, using your own words to phrase your request. [Sixty seconds or more of prayer should go by before we continue. I promise I will wait for you.]

I am now asking for that same permission: "Dear God, my beloved God, Who is the Creator of all that exists; my loving brother Jeshua, who is my spiritual guide and who has given me greater understanding of our Lord; and my loving angels and guides, you who are the messengers of God, I ask all of you for permission to allow me to help in this spiritual healing. I ask that you surround my reader with a white light representing love and spiritual protection, and that you help my reader in opening up his or her heart and soul to receive your blessing, which will aid in his or her spiritual growth. I thank you with all my heart and soul for the permission you are granting me to be able to share these words with this reader, whom I know you dearly love."

Now I ask you, my reader: Is it not true that we live in an incredible moment in time? I speak of this moment, not as if it were a few seconds, a few minutes, or an hour. It can be any period we choose. For this moment of time in which we are together now is such a special one. It is a bridge between the millions and millions of years that have transpired before us and the millions and millions of years that are to come after us. This is a glorious moment, for it connects the infinite past with the infinite future. And now we are sharing this moment in time together on this bridge between the past and the future.

You truly know that the spirit of God resides within you. You know with all your heart and soul that you are a child of God. You know that the greatest gift you have been given is the spirit of God that resides within you. It is the spirit of God that grants you everlasting life and immortality. For truly, since you are the child of our Creator, in reality you are also a part of God.

Just as God gave you the power to create, you also have the power to heal yourself through the spirit of God that resides within you. You have the ability to not only heal yourself spiritually, but also physically. You have the ability to forgive yourself for all of your past acts that may have caused pain or harm to others, for God embraces you totally in providing you forgiveness and love. As God has created the earth as well as our universe, surely you have been given the power, wisdom, and strength to also create in yourself the ability to be at one with God, in spirit as well as in mind.

As we all journey through life, there are many things we have done that have caused us to feel remorse. These may include words or actions that we later recognize have inflicted hurt or damage on some of our brothers and sisters. We truly ask, dear God, that we be able to erase from our souls the marks that have been caused by these actions, marks that have been an expression by us of something other than love or compassion for our brothers and sisters.

If there has ever been a time in your life when you expressed anger, and in doing so, hurt another—and you realize today that you should not have done so—now is the time to forgive yourself. God forgives you, Jeshua forgives you, and your angels and guides forgive you. You are forgiven.

If there has ever been a time in your life when you took advantage of another, knowing it was wrong, now is the time to remove that mark as you proceed in purifying your soul. God forgives you, Jeshua forgives you, and your angels and guides forgive you. You are forgiven.

If there has ever been a time in your life when you criticized another, and in so doing, caused that person pain, now is the time to forgive yourself. God forgives you, Jeshua forgives you, and your angels and guides forgive you. You are forgiven.

If there has ever been a time in your life when you showed a lack of patience toward another, and in so doing, created a scar on your soul, for you hurt that individual as a result of your impatience, now is the time to forgive yourself. God forgives you, Jeshua forgives you, and your angels and guides forgive you. You are forgiven.

If there has ever been a time in your life when you committed an act of selfishness at the expense of another, and in doing so, hurt that individual, now is the time to forgive yourself. God forgives you, Jeshua forgives you, and your angels and guides forgive you. You are forgiven.

If there has ever been a time in your life when you were rude to another, and in that rudeness, caused another pain, now is the time to forgive yourself. God forgives you, Jeshua forgives you, and your angels and guides forgive you. You are forgiven.

If there has ever been a time in your life when you have shown prejudice toward another, and in doing so, hurt that brother or sister, now is the time to forgive yourself. Now is the time to remove that mark from your soul. God forgives you, Jeshua forgives you, and your angels and guides forgive you. You are forgiven.

If there has ever been a time in your life when you lied to another, and in your dishonesty, you brought pain and heartache to that person, now is the time to forgive yourself. God forgives you, Jeshua forgives you, and your angels and guides forgive you. You are forgiven.

If there has ever been a time in your life when another has asked you to be generous and you chose not to bestow this generosity, and it left a scar on your soul, now is the time to forgive yourself. God forgives you, Jeshua forgives you, and your angels and guides forgive you. You are forgiven.

If there has ever been a time in your life when someone has done something for you, and you showed a lack of gratitude that left a mark on your soul because you knew this was not right, now is the time to forgive yourself. God forgives you, Jeshua forgives you, and your angels and guides forgive you. You are forgiven.

If there has ever been a time in your life when a person put out a hand in friendship to you and you chose not to accept it, and you have remorse and sadness within you for not having done so, now is the time to forgive yourself. God forgives you, Jeshua forgives you, and your angels and guides forgive you. You are forgiven.

If there has ever been a time in your life when you have deceived another for your own benefit, and you knew it was wrong and it left a mark on your soul, now is the time to forgive yourself. God forgives you, Jeshua forgives you, and your angels and guides forgive you. You are forgiven.

If there has ever been a time in your life when you showed fear when you should have shown courage, and it left a sadness in your heart and a scar on your soul, now is the time to forgive yourself. God forgives you, Jeshua forgives you, and your angels and guides forgive you. You are forgiven.

If there has ever been a time in your life when you were motivated by greed and, as such, this false value created a hardship for another, now is the time to forgive yourself. God forgives you, Jeshua forgives you, and your angels and guides forgive you. You are now forgiven.

Bring back the memory of any act that you have performed in your life that has caused pain or anguish to another, creating a mark on your soul that still exists. God has now given you permission, Jeshua has given you permission, and your angels and guides have given you permission to forgive yourself for every such act. You are cleansing your entire soul so that your spirit is growing closer and closer to being at one with God. For you truly are a loving child of God, and your Creator wants you to forgive yourself and to be forgiven.

Now that the gates to your heart are open, it is also time to release all that is negatively affecting your soul. You are now releasing all the anger inside of you, regardless of its cause. You are releasing any hatred you have inside your heart and soul, regardless of its cause. You are releasing all negative feelings stored within you, which are poisonous to your heart and soul. You are releasing them now, as well as forever. They are no longer a part of you, and you shall, from this day on, not permit them to be part of you again.

Last, it is time to forgive those you feel have caused you pain. Like you, others have at times created marks on their souls—people who may have lied to you, criticized you unfairly, deceived you, and committed the very same acts against you that you committed against others in the past. They need your forgiveness, just as you have forgiven yourself. They are now forgiven by you.

Your dear beloved Creator, your dear beloved brother Jeshua, and all your angels and guides applaud you, sing praises to you, and congratulate you. For you are releasing all that is negative within your temple of God so that your heart and soul shall be totally pure and will contain only loving thoughts and feelings.

You have now cleansed every mark that was on your soul, so it is fresh with the spirit of God. You have now released all negative things that were within your heart, so that it now only contains those thoughts and emotions that are loving and caring. And now you are making a commitment to live your life from this day on according to "God's will." You are recognizing the need to embrace the laws of God—living your life in universal love, compassion, and truth. And in that recognition, your commitment is pure and genuine. God, Jeshua, and your angels and guides are proud of you and send you their love and blessings.

Moving Forward

Thank you for letting me assist you in receiving forgiveness for that which created a mark on your soul. I, too, have had one on mine, which I am now asking forgiveness for: For many years I had put aside my spiritual mission to instead pursue an endeavor that was motivated by selfishness. For many years I erroneously focused my attention on some very difficult and complex business transactions that would have resulted in substantial income to me, even though Spirit repeatedly told me that I should abandon those efforts and pursue my spiritual mission.

I have now finally done what Oneness asked me to do. I introduced you to my friend Rasha earlier in the book. She has been kind enough to give me Divine guidance from Oneness from time to time, telling me that I am not able to go on my spiritual mission until I give up the pursuit of those selfish business interests. The following is the most recent guidance from Oneness:

> *Rasha, Nick is deep in the enfoldment of his destiny now. The circumstances that continued to thwart his hopes and dreams have been shifted, vibrationally. And the prognosis for the manifestation of the result that is hoped for is very positive. Time is still required to bring about the circumstances in question. And the sense of urgency that colored this effort thus far has waned and given way to a sense of surrender. This was the necessary shift in energy that will allow the momentum of the effort to flow in a natural way.*
>
> *Nick does not require predictions at this point in his process. He requires inner trust. He has put himself in a position of choosing between the voice of fear, instilled by the advice of others . . . and his own sense of a destiny, which is inevitable. The possibility of silencing the negative commentary of others by turning his attention inward is the opportunity at hand now.*
>
> *This is not a drama governed by linear logic. This is a momentum governed by the energy that has brought it into form. The challenge for Nick has been to focus his attention on his own sense of who he knows himself to be. The sense of his true*

identity that will emerge from this adventure will see him on solid ground, despite the illusion that he had journeyed to the edge of a cliff in the material sense.

These are testing conditions through which he will emerge with an unshakable sense of self rather than one attuned to the barometer of the passing winds of change. It is this rudimentary foundation of the indestructible True Self that will be firmly in place as a result of having weathered the storms that shook the illusion of stability to its very foundations.

The intensity of that inner upheaval has subsided now. And there will be a period of floating over the circumstances of day-to-day life that will characterize the present period. There will not be the sense that the inconsequential incidents that may transpire will touch him in the ways he would find important. He will develop a sense of profound detachment from the details of daily life that might once have distracted him and disturbed his sense of inner balance.

Now a sense of inner calm will begin to pervade his being and set the stage for the emergence of another level of beingness. As Nick begins to peel back the layers of who he once was, he will begin to reveal the Source within and become comfortable with it.

It is this newfound sense of identity that will enable him to step forth with grace and wisdom in the wake of circumstances that might otherwise have spurred the aggrandizement of ego. He will know, to the innermost core of his being, that Divinity is at work here. And he will be able to step out of his own way and allow the means for his own spiritual empowerment to be provided, without the inclination to feel that he was in any way personally responsible for it.

He will have realized the levels of humility and gratitude that are necessary to sustain a sense of Presence that is authentic, within the spotlight of the public eye. This profoundly humbling experience of self-scrutiny was the gift in circumstances that had continued to confound him, for in the wording of the illusion—the false identity built on a foundation of material evidence—the possibility of rising to the fullness of who he truly is has been revealed.

This is a time of allowing the dust to settle a bit and for assessing the real assets he holds . . . the ones he holds within. It is the inner self that will support and sustain all he will come to be in this lifetime. For when a world one presumes can be counted on begins to crumble, it is that indestructible inner core that will endure. It is that Source that will serve as a source of strength for others. And it is this that will carry him through the times ahead and into the realms of the timeless . . . a world that has only begun to be revealed to him.

Nick has weathered the virtual annihilation of his own identity and has emerged with much intact. The significance of this profoundly life-altering experience—this inner journey of transformation—will continue to be revealed to him in the days to come.

I am grateful and humbled by the Divine guidance that Oneness has provided me. I am very aware of how wrong it was for me to disregard their guidance these past several years because of my own shortcomings. Again, I now ask for forgiveness from God, Oneness, Jeshua, my loving angels and spiritual guides . . . and myself.

From this day on, I am committed to confining my energy and time to the spiritual mission ahead of me—and to confronting the issues described in the next section of this book.

PART III

The Truth about Jeshua and the Church

Introduction to Part III

As I mentioned in the first part of this book, I grew up in a Catholic neighborhood in a poor blue-collar city: Chelsea, Massachusetts. To my knowledge, I did not meet my first non-Catholic Christian friend until I went to college.

Although I wasn't Catholic myself, I'd often sit in church while my childhood buddies went to confession. I also frequently attended Sunday Masses with them, where they received redemption at Communion for the sins they had allegedly committed the past week. And then they would start the whole process all over again. I found that weekly exercise intriguing.

At Christmastime I enjoyed the beauty and pageantry of Midnight Mass. The friendship and camaraderie was so special to me as I was growing up. And the night before we played our high-school football games, it wasn't unusual for me to join some of my Catholic teammates in going to church and asking God for Divine help in kicking the butts of the team we were to play.

As a child, I was taught to have deep respect and admiration for four very special categories of people: members of the clergy, police officers, teachers, and doctors. And the Catholic priests and nuns were held in the highest esteem out of that group by far. I was in awe of them, admiring the special relationship I knew that they must have had with God.

It wasn't all bliss and joy, though. A number of my friends attended Catholic parochial school before they reached public-high-school age. As I shared with you earlier, it wasn't unusual for them to come home from school and tell me they had been taught by their teachers (who were members of the clergy) that my parents were going to hell when they died because they weren't Christians. I would lie in bed at night crying, and plead with Jesus, "Please don't send my parents to hell." At that time I knew him as Jesus, not Jeshua. Even to this day, when I tell this story in front of an audience, I get choked up with emotion. I'm sure it has left a permanent scar inside of me.

I'm well aware of the substantial humanitarian work performed by the Catholic Church around the world, and I applaud its managers for the charity and relief services that are instituted under its umbrella. The Catholic Relief Services alone provides assistance to millions of people in more than 100 countries.

But I share the information in the rest of this book with a very heavy heart. I only wish that it wasn't necessary to do so and the facts weren't as they are, but it truly is *time for truth.* I realize that you may have a Catholic background and have been taught not to question the teachings of the Church, to accept its doctrines without challenging them, as to do otherwise would be a sin. And because of that training and upbringing, you may be upset by what I am about to reveal to you. Some people may even get angry, accuse me of lying, and feel enormous resentment toward me. I can tell you that it would trouble me greatly if I'm not able to reach those who fall into that category.

As I've expressed earlier, it is not my intent or that of Spirit, who has guided me, to hurt or cause damage to the Church. We—meaning myself and Spirit—truly want to help the Church, to give it an opportunity for "A New Beginning," which is why that is the subtitle of the book. Unfortunately, the leaders of Christianity since the 4th century have done a tremendous disservice to Jeshua. They have distorted his teachings, which has caused the suffering of many millions of people, both those who relied on the

Church for guidance, as well as those who became the victims of its persecution.

Along with the messages of Jeshua, those of Paul, who tried to continue his teachings, have been distorted as well. Jeshua would never have condoned or approved of the following church teachings:

- The existence of a punishing God
- An invented afterlife realm where people suffer eternally if they violate church doctrines
- The notion that all children are born as sinners, condemned by God to go to hell
- The principle that we are responsible for Jeshua's death, because he died for our sins
- The belief that women should be held as inferior to men within the Church

These and many other distortions of the truth will be revealed to you in detail in the remainder of these pages. I am hopeful that this book will fall into the hands of the administrators and managers of the Catholic Church, as well as the other Christian churches. With their understanding and acceptance of the truth, their willingness to take the necessary steps to rectify the situation, and *your* help and support, we truly can change the world we live in. It can be one filled with universal love and compassion, one where we are all recognized as brothers and sisters, for we are all God's children.

Although Part III of this book will undoubtedly be controversial, it's not my intent to alienate anyone, but to help you know the truth about some very important issues. Some of you may weep with joy upon learning these truths, and others may be quite angry, feeling that it is my intent to discredit the Catholic Church. But I have no criticism with respect to the hundreds of millions who practice Christianity or those trained by its leaders and assigned the responsibility of representing it at the regional and local levels who do not know the truth.

My issue is with the leaders of the churches of all Christian denominations who follow the dogmas of the Catholic faith, which is controlled by the Vatican; and more specifically, by the leaders in the Vatican itself. These individuals, who actually dictate the teachings and actions of the Catholic Church, have disseminated false information to their subordinates and followers . . . and continue to do so.

As for my personal beliefs, I've been asked many times as I spoke around the country what religion I am. And my answer is always: "I'm the same religion as God." After letting the questioner stare at me for a few seconds with a confused look, I continue: "What religion do you think God is? Do you think He is a Mennonite or a Quaker? God has no religion, and neither do I."

There is a spiritual relationship that exists between you and God that transcends the religious relationship. I was once told by one of the holiest men in India, Dr. Bindu, whom I wrote about earlier, that when the church or temple is empty, God is not in there. But when you, the child of God, enter, it is you who brings God into the church with you.

As I was accumulating my notes for this section of the book, I became concerned and asked Spirit, "Is it your intent to destroy Christianity?" And the answer came back in gentle words: "Not destroy, but to *save* Christianity."

There are a number of different areas where early Christian leaders intentionally distorted the truth to accomplish their own agenda. In the remainder of this book, we'll explore many of those distortions. Why did these leaders create the concept of hell and the devil? What were the true events leading up to the death of Jeshua, and why did the leaders misrepresent what really took place? What were the results of these falsities and their impact over the last 1,600 years on innocent people around the world?

What really happened to Paul on his way to Damascus, which motivated him to become an apostle? What is the real role that women played in the life of Jeshua and in helping the Apostle Paul with the creation of Christian churches? What were the false justifications used by early Christian leaders to deny their clergy the right to marry and have families? What steps did they take to deny women their rightful place within the church?

And . . . what prompted the *creation* of the Roman Catholic Church in the 4th century? What motivated early Church leaders to have the New Testament translated with hundreds of changes, including the elimination of reincarnation from the Gospels? What is the truth about reincarnation and the role it played in the lives of Jeshua and Paul and in the first several hundred years of Christianity?

The preceding questions, as well as many other important topics, will be discussed in the remainder of *Time for Truth.* And I'll also explore why Church leaders today continue perpetuating those same distortions, and their impact on the world we live in. Not only will I passionately discuss these problems—but *solutions* will also be sincerely offered.

Yes, it is indeed the time for a new beginning! It is time to create a world filled with universal love and compassion.

Chapter 12

The Three Provinces and Paul

Let us now go back 2,000 years, when the Master walked the earth. I want you to visualize what life was like at that time so you have a better understanding of the elements that were in play. This chapter aims to capture the energy, atmosphere, and terrain of the sites known as the Holy Land, as they would have appeared to Jeshua and Paul. What I'm sharing isn't found in the scriptures. This is a special tour that you and I will be experiencing together so we may have a better understanding, both visually and intellectually, of what life was like back then.

At the time, the Holy Land comprised three provinces, bordered on the west by the Great Sea, which today is called the Mediterranean:

1. The northernmost province was **Galilee**, and it was here that Jeshua was raised and lived almost all of his life. While it's true that his mother, Mary, and her husband, Joseph, had lived in Nazareth before his birth, that was not where Jeshua spent his

youth; rather, he resided in the town of Capernaum, along the northwestern shore of the Sea of Galilee.

Galilee was much different from the other two provinces. The only one not occupied by the Romans or part of the Roman Empire, it was a quasi-independent kingdom ruled by Herod Antipas, the son of the Israeli king Herod the Great. Those who wished to cause the Romans trouble in Jerusalem could easily retreat into the hill country of Galilee if they wanted to avoid arrest.

Galilee was indeed a separate entity—politically, geographically, and religiously. It was an agricultural land that grew abundant fruits and vegetables, and it bordered the Sea of Galilee, which had a thriving fishing industry. The fishing trade between Galilee and Jerusalem was very lucrative. Because of the bountiful agriculture there as well as the fishing, Galilee was one of the richest areas in the Holy Land.

A wide dirt road sat elevated above the Sea of Galilee, running parallel to it about 50 yards from its shore. Traveling this road from north to south, one would see the beautiful body of water on one's left, to the east. Although it was known as the Sea of Galilee, in reality it was a lake that was approximately 13 miles long and 7 miles wide. During part of the life of Jeshua, it was called Lake Tiberias, after the Emperor Tiberius. To the right, as one traveled along the road parallel to the lake, were the towns and villages, which included commercial areas and homes, and open rolling hills. It was on one of those hillsides, overlooking the lake, that Jeshua gave the famous Sermon on the Mount.

One of the towns south of Capernaum was Magdala, where the family of Mary Magdalene originally lived before moving to Bethany, outside of Jerusalem. That's why she's called Mary Magdalene, for the people at that time didn't have last names. They were identified by their first name and that of their father—such as Paul, the son of Jacob; or Paul, the son of Abraham. The assumption was that the local residents knew everyone's parents, so the children could be identified in this way, since most likely there would have been more than one Paul living in that area.

If the person came from another location and his father's name wasn't known, he was identified by his home location, such as Paul of Tarsus or Jacob of Alexandria. Since Mary was originally from Magdala, she was known as the Magdalene, just as a person from Boston would be called a Bostonian and one from California a Californian.

2. South of Galilee lay the province of **Samaria**, which had a much less rigid practice of Judaism than Judea, where Jerusalem was located. Foreign armies once occupied Samaria, and many of the soldiers had married local Jewish women and remained there after their tours of duty. The mixed marriages with non-Jews created a much less religious environment.

3. The province of **Judea** lay south of Samaria, and it was where the majority of the population in the Holy Land resided. The Jewish people were actually named after Judea, a region that also included the bustling and exciting city of Jerusalem, which boasted more than 400,000 people. Nazareth was located 70 miles north of Jerusalem; and Bethany, where the Magdalene family lived, lay to the west. To the south could be found Bethlehem, as well as the Hinnom Valley, which included the city dump called Gehenna (which I'll talk about in Chapter 19).

Jerusalem

The city of Jerusalem was separated into two sections by a huge marketplace with hundreds of shops in the center:

1. The wealthier people living in spacious, luxurious homes could be found in the **Upper City**, which had a gentle slope beginning at the marketplace, running in a northwesterly direction.

2. On the southeast side of the marketplace was the **Lower City**, where the poorer people lived. The houses here were very close together, and their roofs were flat, so one could literally walk from one house to another along the rooftops. The homes were heated by braziers, and the glassless windows were so narrow that an intruder couldn't fit through them, yet they allowed air to circulate and had shutters to keep the cold out in the winter.

When Paul arrived in Jerusalem, he became a tenant in a house in the Upper City owned and occupied by a family consisting of a Jewish husband and a Persian wife. When Paul stood in the front yard looking downhill toward the marketplace and the Lower City, he would have seen the following:

His vision, if he glanced left to right, would have first taken in the magnificent Great Temple, with the encompassing Great Wall. Immediately northeast of the temple was the Antonia Fortress, which included the jail Jeshua would have stayed in the night before he was crucified. Farther down the hillside toward the city center was the extraordinary marketplace, which flattened out to accommodate a myriad of activities and included the central shopping area, visited by thousands of people daily.

His eyes would have followed the narrow streets radiating from the marketplace, some moving up the hill toward him and the larger and more luxurious homes. Other roads led away from him to the poorer neighborhoods.

During the day, the marketplace would be bustling, for it was the commercial center of the city. It featured hundreds of retail shops, exotic restaurants, friendly taverns, offices of moneylenders, bakeries, wine shops, and public baths, along with expert tailors, shoemakers, tent makers, artisans and artists, and sellers of merchandise.

Jerusalem was a magical place of rolling hills; large, opulent homes built on the higher ground; and crowded, dirty, noisy, winding streets in the Lower City. It was a place of imported marble, stone, shiny domes, tall spires, and narrow cobblestone streets and alleys. It was a place of Roman aqueducts, busy vendors, verdant gardens, luxurious villas, red earth, gravel paths, and gray stone walls. The wealthier homes featured white marble columns, statues, fountains, atria, and gardens. These properties were often enclosed by white stone walls with gates of iron; and the homes were surrounded by sycamore, carob, pine, and palm trees.

This was the world where Paul lived and Jeshua spent considerable time 2,000 years ago.

Introducing Paul

It's often been said that the Apostle Paul has been written about and spoken of in the Western world more than any person in history other than Jeshua. He is mentioned in almost every service in every Christian church in the world, and his words are the ones most often quoted as part of Christian wedding ceremonies.

Very little is known of the personal life of Paul. It's been assumed by many theologians that he and Jeshua didn't know each other personally, for Paul isn't mentioned in the Gospels, but that isn't true. Paul's name doesn't appear because he wasn't a *disciple,* which meant "pupil." His relationship with Jeshua was one-on-one, very different from that of the disciples. The two were much closer, and discussions were held between them that couldn't have taken place with the disciples, who were not educated men.

Let's take a look at Paul's background. Again, you will not find most of this information in the scriptures.

Paul, whose real name was Paulus, was two years younger than Jeshua. He was born in the region of Cilicia (which today is in Turkey), on the outskirts of the city of Tarsus, which was located on a plain, surrounded by the Taurus Mountains to the north and the mountains of Amanus to the east. The river Cydnus flowed from the Taurus Mountains through a gorge and into the city, and eventually fed into the Great Sea (the Mediterranean), seven miles away. Tarsus was a port of substantial wealth—a great center for learning that included poets, philosophers, and many scholars.

Paul was considered a Roman citizen as a result of his wealthy father having bought this privilege for his family, who were Pharisees, of the Jewish faith. Those having Roman citizenship could look to Rome for help resolving legal disputes, rather than the local authorities, which would save Paul's life in later years. He was educated at home on his father's estate by some of the finest scholars in Tarsus, and was able to speak the language of the Hebrews, as well as Latin and Greek.

As he approached his 18th birthday, Paul relocated to the Holy Land, to Jerusalem, with his father's blessing. He changed his name to its Hebrew equivalent, Saul, so he could fit in more easily with the local people. With funds provided by his father, he began his business career by purchasing shops at the marketplace. He would make payments for them on a monthly basis and rent them out at a higher price to vendors. By buying more stalls, using the same method of financing and receiving income, he increased his wealth and eventually began purchasing land and dividing it into smaller increments. Again, he would pay for it in monthly installments and receive income from tenants who would farm their products on the divided parcels and pay him income in excess of his costs. He was a very successful businessman and was admired for his ingenuity. It's written in the scriptures that he was also a tent maker. This is not true—one of his shops was rented out to a vendor of tents.

In the New Testament, 21 documents are attributed to Paul, and some are in the form of letters, referred to as *epistles*. Four of them are called the *Captivity Epistles,* because Paul stated that he was in prison at the time he wrote them. Three others are known as the *Pastoral Epistles,* because they were addressed to individuals (pastors) rather than to communities. Another seven letters are referred to as the *Catholic Epistles,* because they were written to a community as opposed to individuals (*catholic* in this context means "universal").

As Paul got older, like most aging people, his ability to see close-up became impaired. He began to instruct associates to draft correspondence for him, which they'd subsequently put into their writing style, with their choice of words. This can be easily recognized in his later letters.

In the famous letter written by Paul to the Corinthians, he referred to the "thorn in my flesh," and in his letter to the Romans, several times he spoke of the "weakness" of his "flesh." I have seen theologians variously describe this "thorn" as referring to Paul having been gnomish, hunchbacked, clubfooted, bald with a huge nose, or visually impaired.

None of these descriptions are remotely close to the truth. Paul's "thorn" that he spoke of represented a conflict he had between his flesh and his spirit. Paul was not a married man, and he truly loved the company of women, although he has been wrongly portrayed as a misogynist—one who dislikes women intensely. His conflict was that he demanded that his male church administrators not get involved romantically with the local women, but he himself constantly violated that rule, and he felt guilty over his own lack of self-discipline—thus, the thorn in his side.

As far as his physical appearance is concerned, in a coming chapter you'll find a passage that Christ Consciousness gave to Rasha explaining that when we're incarnated, we find that we're a mixture of many of the lives we previously had. We can sing, dance, or paint a little, perhaps, as well as display a variety of attributes that have been blended together from our past lives. But occasionally a person is born who has been primarily influenced by only one past lifetime. This is seen in child prodigies who can play concert piano at six or seven years old without ever having had a lesson, or paint like a master at an early age.

In my case, I have been told by Spirit and a number of seers (or psychics, if you prefer that term) that in my present incarnation, I have the actual build and facial features of Paul, as well as the skills (or lack thereof) and intellect (or intellectual limitations) that he possessed.

In some areas I am deficient—for example, I couldn't play an instrument if my life depended on it or sing a simple tune such as "Happy Birthday." I'm terrible in the sciences, but in other areas I have been found to be above average. By evaluating *myself,* I have come to know and understand *Paul* very well.

I felt it was necessary that I share this information with you, for we shall now be exploring what is written in the scriptures. I'll explain in further detail those areas that aren't clear. Most important, though, I'll correct the falsehoods that have affected our lives, and in some cases, have been the cause of great suffering and misery.

Chapter 13

What Was Jeshua Really Like?

There's a large part of me that wants to share details about Jeshua—his personality, his emotions, his charisma, his strength, and the essence of who he was. And I've spent the last couple days agonizing over how I should address these points, for it's not the primary purpose of this book. Thus, I am exercising restraint by confining myself to a narrower assignment, although you will get a clear description of Jeshua in this chapter.

One of the responsibilities I've taken upon myself in this book is to give you a greater understanding of how the world really functioned 2,000 years ago. I want to explain some things as simple as the difference between a disciple and an apostle, the attitude of the Jewish people toward their Roman occupiers, and the emotional bond between Jeshua and the Jewish people of that land. But most important, I want to tell you how messages of love were distorted to messages of fear; how messages of compassion were distorted to messages of guilt; and how messages that were supposed to bring us together as God's children instead were so corrupted by early Christian leaders that they polarized people, creating hostilities that persist today with even greater intensity.

The Paintings

Before we begin exploring the events of 2,000 years ago, I do want you to be able to envision what Jeshua looked like. Following my hypnotic regressions, I decided that I'd have a portrait of Jeshua done by a very gifted woman, Rebecca Clark, the daughter of the internationally famous artist and sculptor Lorenzo Ghiglieri.

It was very challenging for me to describe what Jeshua looked like to my talented artist, for I was on the West Coast and she lived in New York at the time. We were constantly sending preliminary drawings back and forth, and I would say, "No, the eyes aren't quite right," or "The hair was slightly different." I finally accepted a finished product from Rebecca, which we were quite pleased with.

Several years later I got a call from a treasured friend of mine, Frank Baranowski (who has since passed away). Frank was an incredibly talented past-life-regression hypnotist whom I once visited in the Phoenix area. He had all the tools of the profession, such as a large, comfortable leather chair for the person being hypnotized to sit in and a microphone that caused his voice to reverberate as he guided you below your conscious mind to your soul mind, where the memories of your previous lifetimes would be retained. He also had a metronome that clicked at a certain speed, inducing you to go more deeply into a hypnotic trance.

And deep I did go. This all happened before the six months of regressions I was to undergo with Julia Ingram that eventually became part of our book, *The Messengers*. In the first scene of 2,000 years ago that I experienced with Frank, I was a young boy of about ten or so, and I was with two other boys slightly older than I was. We were sitting around a table being tutored. I had on a white outfit with white fur trim along the cuffs of my upper garment, as well as on the hem of my short tunic. I thought my family had good taste in clothes.

In the next scene I was sitting on the steep side of a mountain; and there was a fast, rushing river in the valley below. There was also a sheer mountainside on the opposite bank of the river that I could see very clearly. Sitting next to me on a slab of rock was Jeshua. You might be asking how I *knew* this was Jeshua. It would be the same as if I said my father was sitting next to me: I knew who my father was, and I knew who Jeshua was.

In the next scene I was sitting in a tavern, with a man on my right and Jeshua on my left. In front of us was a rough splintered wooden table, almost round, and we had metal or pewter-type vessels in front of us that we were drinking from. Jeshua was telling us a story, and when it was over, the three of us roared with laughter. I remember reaching out with my left hand and putting it on his right forearm. I felt overwhelming love for this man even as I was appreciating his tremendous sense of humor. Other scenes followed, and they were all so moving that I didn't want to come out of the hypnosis.

In addition to being a past-life-regression hypnotist, Frank also hosted a weekly radio program where he interviewed me many times after *The Messengers* came out. He told me that he'd hypnotized more than a thousand people in his life, and our session together was one of the two most memorable experiences he'd had with a client.

That day he called me, Frank's voice was filled with excitement. He said he was going to send me a reproduction of a portrait he'd come across that would have a great impact on me.

The artist was a woman named Bette Myers. One day in 1974, she had what is referred to as a near-death experience after becoming ill. She'd been considered deceased in the hospital, and she explained later that her spirit had traveled through a tunnel and was met by Jeshua.

She was in ecstasy while in his presence, as well as free from all pain associated with her illness. Jeshua instructed her to look at him very closely, and he told her that he was sending her back to her body and wanted her to paint his portrait. Bette reluctantly returned and was revived.

Ten years later while in her studio with a client, she suddenly felt compelled to begin the portrait that Jeshua had asked her to paint. She completed it that same afternoon, after just 135 minutes. The portrait is beautiful, but what is amazing—the reason why Frank was so excited—is that it's obviously the face of the same person Rebecca had painted for me. In Bette's painting he is facing the viewer at a slightly different angle, and there are some other minor differences based on the two artists' painting styles and use of colors, but indeed it is the same person: Jeshua.

One day Rebecca came to my office and looked at her painting and a copy of the one done by Bette Myers side by side on the wall behind my desk. She said without any hesitation and with great excitement, "Nick, the same person modeled both paintings! It is definitely the same person!"

Here are the two paintings so that you may know what Jeshua looked like:

Rebecca's painting of Jeshua.

A print of the above portrait, which is by Bette Myers, can be purchased at **www.bettemyersart.com** or by calling 877-347-6289.

I now keep both Rebecca's original painting and the Bette Myers reproduction in my home. I'm so grateful for the many hours I spent under past-life regression, for the paintings allow me to remember Jeshua so vividly.

Jeshua Teaches

I was motivated several years ago to write a historical novel of the life of Paul called *The Commitment.* I basically did so using my soul memory—in other words, I wrote it through the memory of Paul, placing my own conscious mind aside. It includes many wonderful conversations and sermons from Jeshua that have never been heard before, for they're not found in the New Testament.

I never submitted my manuscript to a publisher, but I did send it to my six test readers. Afterward, they persuaded me to take a chapter describing Jeshua's sermons and include it in this book. You'll find it in the following pages.

You'll notice that some concepts I may have shared with you earlier in this book originated from the words of Jeshua remembered through my soul memory. Jeshua has greatly influenced my life today, just as he did Paul's 2,000 years ago.

Here is that chapter from my manuscript *The Commitment.* (By the way, as I mentioned earlier, Paul went by the name Saul while he lived in Jerusalem.)

Saul entered the grounds of the temple through its southern gate, into the Court of the Gentiles. The sun had not reached its full height, and since it was the colder time of year, he knew that Jeshua would be speaking in front of the crowd on the south-facing side of the temple, where the temperature would be warmer, as opposed to in the shade. As Saul approached the stairs, he saw that many hundreds of people had gathered, some sitting on the marble stairs and some milling around the landing below. There were people of all descriptions, and unlike the earlier days when Jeshua had begun speaking, it appeared to Saul that approximately a quarter of the people gathered were women.

Saul thought, The people here are truly a cross-section of Jerusalem. There were elderly men with long white beards, and others dressed like fairly well-to-do professional people, both men and women. Those standing on the periphery appeared to have the bearing and attire of members of the religious authorities, and were joined by their scribes. There were also poorer people. Some were shoeless, wearing ill-fitting tunics, stained and in need of mending—in contrast to those of the wealthier class, who were dressed festively, as though they were attending a social gathering.

Saul noticed there were no children, but the women as a whole appeared to be younger than most of the men, probably in their late teenage years or early 20s.

Even though the courtyard behind Saul was referred to as the Court of the Gentiles, where the pagans were allowed to sell their birds and other small animals to the Jews for sacrifice, he noticed that the crowd appeared to be made up only of Jewish people. It made sense to Saul that very few Gentiles, who believed in pagan gods, would have had an interest in hearing what Jeshua had to say.

Saul recognized only a handful of people he knew, and soon the assembled crowd in his estimation had to number several hundred. It was at this time that Jeshua appeared, even though no one had noticed his entrance into the courtyard and his approach. Unlike every other time—when Jeshua had addressed his audience standing below them on the marble slab in front of the stairs, with the people on the stairway—he climbed the stairs so he was now standing very close to the top, where he could look down upon all the people.

Saul positioned himself to Jeshua's right, approximately six steps lower than his friend. The crowd was so enormous that it was impossible for him to make eye contact with Jeshua. There was tremendous excitement among the crowd, with the sounds of hundreds of people talking simultaneously as they began to arrange themselves in a fan shape around Jeshua.

Jeshua looked magnificent, standing with great serenity, with the sun creating golden highlights in his hair. He was wearing an off-white robe made of very soft material that fell just above his ankles. Its sleeves were open and stopped above his wrists. His eyes were clear, and his face radiated both strength and beauty as he silently looked over his audience.

Several minutes went by during which it got quieter and quieter, until there was total silence. And now Jeshua began to speak in a melodious voice that was resonant, yet filled with so much passion that it felt as if he were talking personally to each individual.

He began: "Everything that is important to you in life, including your need to be loved and accepted, is contained within you. Everything that you need, in trying to understand your relationship with God, lies within. For within you is a storeroom that contains many wonderful things. Each of you has a key that will open the door to that storeroom. You may enter it and take what is yours and visit it as often as you choose to, once you understand that it is a gift that you all have received in being part of God."

Jeshua waited a few seconds so that what he was saying could be processed by the people. He looked around at his audience and then continued: "There is an internal wisdom and spiritual mind that most times you refrain from trying to communicate with. Yes, it is difficult to center yourself within your spiritual mind so you are in tune with it. But if you are not aware of it, or at best, if you are not making an effort to be in touch with it, it is impossible to become at one with it, which is what brings happiness and understanding. It will become obvious to you that there are so many things that you worry about in life that are immaterial, for they have nothing to do with happiness.

"So you must look within, for the greatest gifts you have are internal. You must <u>learn</u> to center yourselves. You must learn how to find your soul mind. If you open a channel, you shall see and shall understand, for it is within every one of you who are God's children."

Saul turned his head and looked at the faces of the people standing below him and saw that they were enraptured. The words of Jeshua were making a tremendous impression on them, and Saul could see that Jeshua's messages were greatly touching their souls.

Another voice, one that was strong, boomed out at Jeshua: "Rabbi [teacher], I have heard you say before that we have the gift of free will. How does that affect our ability to become at one with God?"

Jeshua looked in the direction of the questioner. He purposely waited a few moments and then answered in a voice filled with passion, strength, and love: "God gave you the free will to choose your own path on your way to reaching your destiny. The path that many of you have chosen, unfortunately, leads you farther and farther away from God, as well as from truth, and now there are many of you who are lost.

"So many of you have been led astray by pleasures of the senses, as well as your desire for gain in the material world. You must realize that the material world itself can only give you gifts that are temporal and have nothing of lasting value. The kingdom of heaven lies within you, and God is within you, also, residing within your own soul. You are part of one great spiritual family, for every one of you is a child of God. You must understand that and try to develop a feeling of unity, knowing that indeed we are all one and are manifestations of God."

Jeshua then broke into a beautiful smile, and his eyes shone brightly as he continued: "Live in peace, live in love, and be aware of the presence of God at all times. God is here, and you have the spirit of Him residing within you, which gives you your divinity, as it does all your brothers and sisters, so you must have love and compassion for all."

A woman's voice could then be heard coming from one of the bottom stairs, near the marble slab. She asked, "Jeshua, what is the most important emotion or feeling we can have—is it peace or friendship?"

Jeshua took one step down, as if he was trying to come into closer contact with the woman who had asked the question. And then he answered: "Love is the motivating force for the world, for love is God. Let love flow from you and see its illuminating power. The power of God through love transcends everything and can bring peace and tranquility to the troubled world.

"The laws of God are so simple. I say to each and every one of you, my brothers and sisters, it is so easy to understand what God is asking of you. And you do not need the permission of any other individual in order to accept the laws of God, nor do you have to pay another individual, whether it be a priest or anyone else in the temple, in order to live this truth.

"What God is asking of each and every one of you is that you embrace love and compassion for all and live your lives in truth. If you are willing to do that, then surely you will realize that you are at one with God and will touch the lives of so many people, that they may also enjoy life through you."

A man yelled out: "How about the priests, Jeshua? They tell us that God is found through them—through their teachings and their efforts—through their animal sacrifices, the tithing that we pay them, and the rituals that they teach us. They say that God is found here, in this temple. How do you respond?"

A silence fell over the crowd, for they knew that Jeshua's answer might challenge the power and influence of the religious authorities and the temple. Jeshua, in a very soft but firm voice, answered: "You are the temple of God. If God resides within you, is it not true that you may hold your services with God anytime you choose, whether it be as you walk through a field; as you are lying down on your own bed; as you are shopping in the marketplace; and, yes, as you take your temple into the temple that stands behind me?

"But God does not care about rituals. God does not care if you stand up or sit down while you are praying to Him. Nor does He ask you to memorize words, which come from your mind rather than from your heart."

The crowd and Jeshua heard a voice cry out, a stern voice, as if it belonged to one of the priests: "Have you come to judge us?"

A few moments went by before Jeshua answered. "I stand as an individual in the presence of God. I have come not to judge you, but to help you. I have come not to judge the world, but to save the world."

With that, a commotion broke out: the voices of hundreds of people talking at once, responding to what Jeshua had just said.

One voice filled with hope and respect then called out: "Jeshua, I have heard of the healings that you have done in Galilee and Samaria. Will you be doing healings here in Jerusalem?"

Jeshua answered, "Yes, God's love for you will be manifested here in Jerusalem, also. The healings are done to show the power of God that is contained within you and the love that God has for you, His children. I am the conduit for God.

"I will be in the marketplace in the Lower City, at the main well at full sunrise. Tell those who seek to be healed and who have faith and belief in the power of God's love to come and

join me. I leave you now, but I shall return in two days on these temple stairs and share more of God's messages with you."

Having said that, Jeshua began to walk down the stairs. The crowd parted for him, creating a pathway. As he walked past, many reached out and touched his arm or a piece of his clothing.

Saul could see the faces of the people. Most were enraptured, having been tremendously moved by the words Jeshua shared. The crowd began to follow Jeshua, closing ranks behind him as he headed across the Court of the Gentiles and through the exit adjacent to the Royal Portico.

Saul stood on the stairway and watched the scene with great pride; and finally when Jeshua was no longer in sight, he began to work his way through the people, down the stairway, and into the courtyard.

He eventually made his way to the Lower City and found a small table at the bazaar, where he enjoyed a quiet meal by himself. He was deep in thought and preferred not to have any company, but rather to process the event he had just witnessed and try to envision what would take place later that afternoon in the marketplace. Yes, he thought, that afternoon would be an extraordinary experience for all present. . . .

I hope that the excerpt I have provided from my manuscript *The Commitment* has enabled you to grasp the essence of Jeshua: his charisma, energy, compassion, and love for others. I hope that it has given you a greater understanding of the impact he had on people and how he was able to influence their lives in such an incredibly positive way. And that charisma, compassion, and love still live on today.

Chapter 14

JESHUA OF TODAY

I had serious reservations as to whether I should share the following story with you. After much contemplation, I decided I would tell it to you exactly as it happened, letting you process it and come to your own conclusions about it, as well as how it could potentially affect the world we live in.

In 1996, I spent some time with a group of people in Europe with whom I had many discussions of a business and social nature. One of the members of the group was Anna, a very sophisticated, intelligent, bilingual European woman who had traveled the world.

In September 2007, I received a totally unexpected phone call from Anna, whom I hadn't talked to in probably six or seven years. There was excitement in her voice, and after we went through the usual polite inquiries, she told me the reason for her call: She'd been assisting someone who was extraordinary beyond measure. She said that there was no other like him in the world. And she said that he wanted to talk to me, that he *knew* me.

As she described him, it appeared to me that she was almost embarrassed to identify him by name, but I finally asked her, "Are you talking about Jeshua?"

I could hear her breath catch, and after a few seconds, she quietly said, "Yes." She told me that being in his presence was the most extraordinary experience of her life. That his charisma was beyond description. That his love and understanding and wisdom were beyond words. She'd been working for him at that point for more than four years, arranging meetings and delivering and receiving documents for him in various countries.

Anna also told me that he spoke the language of every place they had visited, including different dialects. She let me know the date he wanted me to call him, which was four days later, and gave me his phone number.

After we said good-bye, I sat for a while trying to absorb what she'd told me. I had never known her to lie, but I felt I should try to use every resource I could think of to confirm the validity of what she'd shared before I made my phone call to this man—whom I shall refer to as J as I continue telling you what transpired.

Confirmation by Sara

I have several acquaintances whom I consider to have a special relationship with God, Spirit, and the angels that goes far beyond mine. One of them is Sara O'Meara, whom I do consider a living saint. As I wrote in an earlier chapter, I've seen Sara perform many miracles, such as the healing of hundreds of people while she prayed for them. She is a person whose credentials—including Nobel Prize nominations four years in a row for her humanitarian work—are impeccable.

Sara is also like a sister to me. I called her and told her everything that Anna had told me, and then I asked if she would confer with her angels about whether this man was indeed Jeshua. Sara told me that she suspected the chances were extremely remote, but she would ask, although I should prepare myself for disappointment. We both acknowledged that Anna was most likely wrong about the man's identity, in spite of how certain she'd been.

Sara called me back the following morning. I could hear the excitement in her voice as she said, "Nick, my angels told me that this man you will be talking to is indeed a facet of Jeshua."

We then discussed what that meant—that he was a "facet" of Jeshua. We used a diamond as our illustration: If one were to chip off a portion of a diamond, it would be said to reveal a *facet* of that diamond. Perhaps another word might be *part*. So the man embodied part of Jeshua.

Sara asked me to promise that I would share what occurred in my conversation with him, and I told her I would.

Confirmation by Rasha

In addition to Sara, I also contacted another extraordinary person, Rasha, who transcribes the teachings of a Divine source, as I told you about in Chapter 3. As I mentioned, from time to time Rasha has e-mailed me channeled messages that Oneness has given to her, such as the one that appeared in Chapter 11. They're always profound, and I've kept them as a special collection.

I called Rasha, who was currently visiting the U.S., and told her about my phone conversation with Anna. I asked her if she would allow herself to go to that special meditative place in her mind she visits when she connects with Oneness and writes down their messages.

Rasha told me she would ask a Divine source that she sometimes refers to as The Christ if there was a willingness to answer my question. That evening I received a very unexpected call from Rasha. When she had gotten off the phone with me, she felt drawn to drive to the rural village of Chimayó, New Mexico, and the legendary Santuario de Chimayó, a chapel known for the miracles that reportedly occur there.

She told me she had received the answer from The Christ that I was seeking and had taken it down in longhand. She said the information was extraordinary and promised to e-mail it to me that same evening.

I thought for a long time about whether I should give you the entire message from The Christ, for a portion of it is personal, in that it pertains to me only. It's embarrassing for me to include it, as it is information that I would normally keep to myself. But I've been told by Spirit that I should reprint it exactly as it was given to Rasha, and not delete anything. So the following is the message from The Christ through Rasha:

> [I was asked to get your verification for Nick Bunick of the identity of a man with whom he has been connected. He believes that this man could be the reincarnation of Jeshua. I ask you to comment on the validity of this claim, if possible.]
>
> *The information you seek cannot be revealed in the way the question has been presented. For it must be understood that the linear disposition toward the reemergence of consciousness in human form does not transpire in the manner you assume it does. One undergoes a fragmentation of past awareness in the process of reemerging in human form. And the aspects of one's consciousness that held a particular identity of the past may merge with those of their other lifetimes.*
>
> *An individual may indeed contain a fragment of the essence of a particular identity—one who could be said to have lived before—and that being could indeed harbor the full archive of the memories amassed during the lifetime in question, yet those impressions would also be colored, in the present individual's core essence, by other fragmentations, other lifetimes, other identities.*
>
> *Many will emerge who believe themselves to be the direct reincarnation of the being you refer to as Jeshua. Each will present his own unique combination of variables within the mix in which that Essence is also present. And dependent upon the unique combination of those variables, an individual may or may not be able to manifest the full potential, in this lifetime, that lies dormant and is inherent in the Essence carried forth into the Now.*
>
> *The individual in question has risen to an exceptional level of self-recognition and carries the full capacity to transform humanity through the touch of his Presence. Whether or not he will succeed in this is a matter no less of personal will than of*

personal destiny. The intentions of all concerned are surely honorable. No malice of will is involved in this connection. Nick may feel he is called to manifest his destiny through this association, and well he may do so. But the destiny made manifest would be his own, and not be dependent upon this individual, or upon anyone.

Each of the men has the capacity to rise to the fullness of the potential inherent in each of them to bring to completion an exercise in "Divinity made manifest" that was implanted within the consciousness of humanity many thousands of years ago. It was for this possibility that each of them has answered the inner calling to claim that aspect of themselves and to re-create a focus on a drama that cries out—universally—for completion in these times.

That same theme—the energy of that same drama—will manifest within many, as the seed of that ancient fragment of consciousness takes root and begins to blossom within the awareness of those in whom it is implanted. The form each of those manifestations will take will differ. Some will come to fruition as foreseen, and some will be abandoned in midcourse. Yet the energy that serves as the impetus to action within each of these seeds of Divine Intent spurs the drive to completion of the mission to which they are so deeply and timelessly invested.

The call of the inevitable has been heard in the inner depths of the one who thinks of himself as Nick. He has responded accordingly. He has been empowered by his own deviation from the identity he believed himself to embody. Life will take astounding and unexpected turns from this point forth as he begins to explore the truth of who he is and what he has brought to these times as an investment in Divine consciousness made manifest.

We are The Christ—bridging time—coming forth into the Now in this way as an affirmation of what is already known and is harbored within you. Be at peace with the inkling of self-recognition—for it is merely one of many clues that will be provided along the way.

The Conversation with J

It was now time for me to make my phone call to J. Anna had given me the name he goes by in this lifetime, which is European sounding, but she always referred to him as Jeshua. I decided I would avoid calling him by name until he gave me some indication as to whether he wanted me to know and believe he was Jeshua. This concern didn't last very long after I dialed the overseas number.

J answered, and I introduced myself. He responded with a kind laugh and said, "Nick, you have the same exact voice you had 2,000 years ago." His own voice was gentle but firm, with the ever-so-slight trace of an accent I couldn't identify. The next words he said caught me totally by surprise: "Two thousand years ago I lost my temper, and it cost me my life. I can't let that happen again."

He then asked me to let him talk for a while, and proceeded to tell me how saddened he was over the conditions existing in the world today. He said that 2,000 years ago we'd given people our messages, but they had gotten lost. This time we should present them again and teach people how to live by them. However, he told me that our first priority was humanity. He said, "Parents cannot think of their relationship with God when they have hungry children they can't feed or lack clean water for them to drink. Taking care of those in need who are suffering and struggling in the world is our first responsibility, and then we will be able to care for their souls."

J and I discussed a number of things that afternoon, including how his death came about. It's important that you process the following account carefully, for it's so different from what has been taught for the last 1,600 years. In chapters to come, I'll also be discussing many events in the lives of Jeshua and Paul, including "facts" that have been given to us that are false. What J told me on the phone provided me with an understanding of other elements that were in play 2,000 years ago.

He told me that the morning after the night he was arrested, he was taken before Pontius Pilate, who was the Roman governor of Judea appointed by Caesar. There were three additional elderly

Jewish men in his chamber. They were members of the Sanhedrin, a group of 70 men who were the overseers of the Jewish religion in the Holy Land. Contrary to the Gospels, there had been no trial of Jeshua the night before by this Jewish council. Pilate had summoned three members as witnesses.

Pilate then turned on Jeshua, verbally attacking him, accusing him of preaching that there was someone in the Holy Land more powerful than the emperor. Jeshua responded by trying to explain to Pontius Pilate that he wasn't talking about a mortal but someone outside of this realm, his God. Pilate became very angry at him, repeating his accusations.

Jeshua, in turn, also got angry and asked Pilate why he couldn't understand what Jeshua was saying—that it was not a person, but *God* he had been referring to in his talks. But the only gods Pontius Pilate could relate to were the wooden and plaster idols that the Romans prayed to, and they certainly weren't considered superior to the emperor.

The two began shouting at one another. Pilate turned to the three elderly Jewish men and said, "See how he is talking to me?" He then turned back to Jeshua and demanded that he acknowledge that he was wrong and that no one was greater than the emperor.

Jeshua basically told Pilate that he couldn't believe how ignorant the man was not to understand that he wasn't talking about another human being. They again began to yell at one another.

Pilate shouted, "Enough!" He turned to his guards and told them to take Jeshua out of his chamber and have him replace one of the three prisoners who were to be crucified that morning.

J told me that the three elderly Jewish men said they wanted nothing to do with this. They went over to a basin and began to pour water over their hands, which is an old Jewish custom signifying they didn't want any part of what was going on. It's interesting to note that in the scriptures, it's claimed that Pilate was the one who washed his hands, implying *he* didn't want to be responsible for Jeshua's death, but that there was an angry mob of Jews outside demanding he have Jeshua killed. This was a total fabrication by the early Christian leaders.

One of the last things J told me before we said good-bye was that when he finished his mission on Earth, another "facet" of him would take his place while he went on to other realms.

Confirmation by the Angels

I spent a few hours the rest of the afternoon and into that evening processing the conversation. I could hear J's voice in my mind, his gentle laugh, and the profound words he shared with me. The next day I had a phone appointment with a woman who has a rare gift. She has requested that I use a fictitious name, so I'll call her Janet. Janet has the unique ability to see and talk to angels, who provide answers to questions people ask them through her. Allow me to give you an example of the gift that Janet has been given by Spirit.

To talk to Janet, people have to make a phone appointment with her, write down their questions on a piece of paper, and state that they are giving the angels permission to answer their questions. One time a few years ago I called her on a Thursday night and asked if she had any information for me from the angels.

She told me that they were showing her suitcases and a map and said that I'd be taking a trip to London. Even though I hadn't said a word about it to Janet, indeed I had plane tickets to London for that coming Sunday. She then told me the angels were showing her that I would be going from London to Geneva. I felt I finally caught them in an error, for I had absolutely no plans to go to Switzerland. Janet assured me I would meet a man in Geneva, and we would become good friends. She described the man in detail and gave me his initials.

Three days later I left for London. After I was there one day, I got a call from a man in Brussels, Belgium, whom I'd been in touch with months earlier, asking me to meet with him and three other men in Switzerland. They were flying in to discuss a business opportunity in Geneva.

When I arrived in Geneva, I immediately went to the hotel where we'd agreed to meet and took a seat on a comfortable sofa in the large lobby. Within an hour the four men arrived, and one sat down next to me. He told me his name, which had the same initials that Janet had mentioned, and he precisely matched the description she had given me. And he and I did become good friends for many years.

The story I've just recounted is 100 percent true and is just one of many, many dozens I can tell you attesting to Janet's gift. And now, here I was calling her to see what information I could learn about the experience I'd had on the phone with J the day before.

After Janet and I exchanged pleasantries, she said a little prayer (as she always does) in a voice totally different from her own, inviting the angels to join her and participate in the session. I told her that I'd talked to a man the day before on the phone who I believed might have been Jeshua.

I'd barely finished the sentence when Janet jumped in and said, "Yes, the angels are telling me he *is* Jeshua!"

I related what J had said about the reason why he'd died 2,000 years ago, and without my saying another word, she proceeded to repeat the exact same story he had told me, which she said the angels were relaying to her.

Janet and the angels also told me I would be traveling around the world with J, visiting Lourdes and other places, but that we wouldn't be allowed to go to Israel because of tensions existing at that time. She also told me that the angels had asked her to make sure I understood that I should eat and sleep whenever I could when I was with J, for he doesn't require food or rest.

That evening I tried to piece it all together. In addition to J's own words, I had confirmations of his identity from Sara, who had asked her angels; from Rasha, who had received information from The Christ; and from Janet, who had spoken with *her* angels.

That phone call with J took place in the latter part of 2007. I had other conversations with him, as well as receiving an invitation to come spend time with him overseas, but we then decided to delay our first visit until he comes to the U.S. It's not unusual for me to talk to Anna almost every other week, but rarely with J, for he is constantly traveling throughout Europe, Asia, and other parts of the world.

Anna's Observations

Anna has told me some remarkable stories. She said that she and J never travel together. When they have to go to another country, he tells her he'll meet her, and she has no idea how he gets there. If indeed he is Jeshua, I am guessing it's possible for him to go into the spiritual world from wherever he is, and then come back to this dimension in whatever city and country he chooses. Anna has no idea where he stays—it's not at the hotel she checks into, and he never tells her where. She also confirmed that he never eats or sleeps.

Anna said that one time he showed up at her hotel in a country she had just traveled to, and when she met him, she was in shock: he was three to four inches taller than he'd been before! When he noticed she was staring at him, he asked her why, and she told him. He laughed and said it wasn't intentional, and in a flash he was back to his normal height.

I'm again guessing that it's possible that when he traveled from here to the spirit world and then back to his destination in this dimension, he accidentally came back a different height. Anna mentioned that he seemingly never ages and appears to be in his mid-30s.

She also told me that he had disappeared for several weeks around Easter of 2008. She wasn't able to locate him anywhere or reach him at any phone number she had or by e-mail. J finally reappeared and seemed uncomfortable. When she asked him where he'd been, he took off his shirt and showed her that his body had slash wounds, as if he had been beaten with a whip or other instruments. He also removed his shoes and showed her that he had the stigmata wounds on his feet and palms, like Jeshua would have experienced at the crucifixion. He had gone away by himself to heal. That was the only year out of the five Easters they had known each other that these mysterious events had occurred. Anna and I discussed this but couldn't come up with an explanation.

I can't say with absolute certainty that the man I've described to you is Jeshua. I have no right to make such an assertion. It doesn't matter what opinion *I* have, because the consequences if he *is* Jeshua are so great that I wouldn't make such a claim unless I was 100 percent positive, without even a shadow of a doubt.

If he is indeed Jeshua, how does he go about letting the world know he is here on Earth? Through what medium does he do so? How does he appear publicly without being accosted by thousands of people at every turn? And how would he protect himself against a deranged person who might wish to take his life, or extremists who allege that he's a fraud and want to take matters into their own hands?

If J is Jeshua, I feel it's not my right or privilege to answer the many questions you would undoubtedly have for him. Only *he* has that right, and you can form your own judgments. But he did help clear up some points for me regarding what happened 2,000 years ago.

Let's move on to the next chapter and explore Jeshua's birth, life, and death. You will learn of the dire consequences arising from the Catholic Church's portrayal of the circumstances of his death, which have had devastating effects on the lives of millions of people.

Chapter 15

Jeshua's Life and Death

Mary was 16 years old when Jeshua was born. Her husband, Joseph, was 20 years older than she was. Although it wasn't unusual in Judea for a girl to marry that young, it's still strange that she would wed a man so much older. Also, one would assume that a man that age most likely would have had a previous marriage, one in which perhaps his wife had passed away. These questions are never addressed in the scriptures. Instead, Mary is described in the original scrolls as being an *almah,* which could mean either a young woman or a virgin.

Was there a virgin birth? Even Jeshua would not have known the answer to that question. It was one the Catholic leaders fought over for hundreds of years. Does it really make a difference? Whether he was born of a virgin or not doesn't change who Jeshua was either way. But certainly it would have made a difference in the attitude of Mary and Joseph *toward* Jeshua.

And if indeed there had been three Magi who traveled across the continent to be present at his birth in Bethlehem, as reported in the Gospels, why would they have then abandoned him?

Wouldn't these three men of great wealth who appeared in order to welcome God's child have continued to monitor his life, and perhaps even have provided guards for him for security when he was growing up? Wouldn't they perhaps have moved him and his family to a more luxurious setting, rather than his being raised in a remote town in northern Galilee?

At the Council of Nicaea in the 4th century, the Christian leaders wanted to assure that Jeshua would be considered a deity, the son of God. How better to achieve this than to have the Gospels claim that there was a miraculous virgin birth and that three Magi had followed a star and witnessed this event while angels were singing. It is apparent that Jeshua and Paul had no knowledge of these claims. Jeshua taught that we are *all* God's children.

I have no reservations accepting that Jeshua was born as the unique, beloved son of God . . . that he had reached perfection prior to his birth and is part of God, as we all are. He was born at the top of the pyramid, at one with God and Christ Consciousness. He *was* Christ Consciousness. It is most likely that he had lived previous lifetimes in which he ascended the stairs until he reached this state. It is even stated in the scriptures that when he was preaching in a temple, he was asked how he could know so much, considering how young he was. And he responded that before Abraham was, *he* was. This would imply he had lived a previous lifetime before that of Abraham.

Every so often an avatar is born on Earth, one whose spirit is pure, whose wisdom is extraordinary, and who becomes a great teacher and whose life becomes an example for all to emulate. I believe that Jeshua went beyond even those criteria, with or without a virgin birth, and with or without the appearance of the Magi and the angels singing.

The Disciples

As I've already mentioned, contrary to the scriptures, Jeshua did not grow up in Nazareth—instead, he lived in Capernaum, which is located in the central part of the province of Galilee, on the Sea of Galilee. Visualize him walking along the shores of this beautiful lake, watching the fishermen working their nets and the farmers toiling in the fields. Also contrary to the scriptures, he didn't develop a trade as a carpenter. In many of his parables, he makes reference to the products that grow in the ground or are found in the waters of the lake, but never to anecdotes associated with carpentry.

In fact, the first seven men he recruited to join him had been fishermen who also lived in towns along the coast. These were not educated men, for less than 10 percent of the entire population in the Roman Empire could read or write. They became known as *disciples,* a word that comes from the Latin *discipulus,* which means "pupil." And indeed, they were his pupils, whom he had to teach using simple words so they could understand his messages.

But were there only 12 pupils he shared his knowledge with? Of course not. During the years he walked the earth, Jeshua had hundreds of disciples he taught and preached to, scattered among the three provinces of Israel. It's interesting to note that the Catholic Church would have you believe that his disciples had only been men. And this is not true. Jeshua had many female pupils who revered and loved him and were totally devoted to him.

But in the 4th century when the scriptures were carved in stone, the Christian leaders made sure that no women were mentioned as disciples. Perhaps that's why they reduced the number of disciples to 12, for if they had instead acknowledged that he had hundreds, it would have been impossible for them to claim that none of them had been women.

The function of Jeshua's early disciples, those who were fishermen from Galilee, was to travel with him to provide safety and ensure that they all were able to find the necessities to accommodate their needs. Some would be sent out in advance, knowing that Jeshua would be in a certain town within the next two days. They would arrange shelter for him during that visit, as well as food and any other requirements. Traveling on foot from Capernaum to the towns to the south, through the hills and desert land in the province of Samaria, was a difficult and tiring journey. It could also be dangerous, since being attacked for one's possessions wasn't unusual as one ventured through the remote areas.

Jeshua's Mission

The Gospels are silent as to how Jeshua spent a good part of his life, from childhood until the last several years before his death. During that time, he traveled throughout the Holy Land, teaching and preaching, trying to help people understand the answers to the same two questions I posed to you earlier in this book: *What is the purpose of our lives?* and *What is our relationship with God?*

He taught them . . .

- . . . that they should live in love and be aware of the presence of God at all times, that the kingdom of God was within them, and that the spirit of God inside them gave them their divinity.
- . . . that they were all Divine children and that love was the motivating force in their world, for love *was* God.
- . . . that the power of love, through God, transcends everything and could bring peace and calmness to their troubled world.
- . . . that each of them could become a messenger of love and light and spread this truth so that others might also change their way of living and overcome the difficulties that at times overwhelmed them.
- . . . that God's spirit was within them, residing within their own being; that God was everywhere; and that they were part of one great spiritual family, children of God, brothers and sisters.

He encouraged them to develop feelings of unity, of oneness, knowing that indeed they were all manifestations of their beloved God.

What happened to those teachings of Jeshua? How did they get transformed into fear-inducing testaments? Why were others later taught, as some still are now, that they would be punished by God if they failed to adhere to the Church doctrines?

It is because early Christian leaders concluded that it was easier to control the lives of people that way. The Roman Empire consisted of 80 million people. Wasn't it easier to manipulate the minds of their citizens through fear rather than with swords and brute force—and certainly not with love?

But if force was necessary, as displayed over hundreds of years during the Inquisitions, didn't it make sense to punish and maim the nonbelievers, and when they were through torturing them, send them on their journey to the hell that their religion had created for them?

The Gospels portray the time before the final years of Jeshua's life as "missing," when in reality he had begun his mission in earnest. But it was in the last several years that he began to perform miracles, such as healing the sick, similar to those done today by my dear friend Sara O'Meara. There are just a handful of people on Earth today—and perhaps Jeshua was the only one in *his* time—endowed with that special gift: the Divine privilege to be able to reach that part of God inside of those who need healing, and ask the Almighty to restore wellness to body and mind.

Many times the sickness was caused by people's own marks on their souls, from acts they committed that weren't consistent with God's will. I am referring to displays of selfishness, bigotry, revenge, hate, dishonesty, thievery, cruelty, and anything else that would have created negative karma for them. And Jeshua would pray for them and ask them to feel sincerity and true remorse, and to accept forgiveness from God and from their own essence (as you and I did together in the chapter on forgiveness). In so doing, they would release the negative karma and be healed.

The scriptures portray these people as being possessed. You would have thought half the population of Jerusalem was plagued by demons—evil spirits that the Catholic Church created along with their apparent parent, the devil. But the real word, coming from Greek literature of 500 years earlier, was *daemons,* which referred to undesirable traits, not evil spirits. And Jeshua taught his most advanced pupils—or disciples, if you prefer—how to pray for these people and touch their hearts and minds, as I described, so they could also help heal themselves.

During the time Jeshua was performing his mission in the Holy Land, great tension existed between the Jews and the Romans. At the time of his birth, the Romans had already occupied the region for more than 50 years. They were tremendously well entrenched, particularly in the province of Judea. Many of the streets had been paved to accommodate their horses and chariots. It wasn't uncommon to hear the rhythmic sound of steel-tipped boots coming in contact with cobblestone as the Roman soldiers marched or jogged in formation through the streets of Jerusalem.

The primary, and perhaps only, reason for the Roman occupation was the collection of taxes from the Jews. The wealth of the Roman government was principally generated by the monies they demanded from the countries they occupied, and Judea was no exception. They would tolerate the Jewish people practicing their own religion, but they acted swiftly and cruelly whenever they felt that the authority of Rome was being challenged. Just four years before the birth of Jeshua, in response to hostility on the part of some Jewish people, the Romans destroyed a number of villages and crucified more than 2,000 Jews in order to set an example.

Jeshua felt great pain for the suffering of the Jewish people at the hands of the Romans. But he also realized that he couldn't accept a role in expelling the Romans from their land, contrary to the expectations of the local people. His interests lay not in saving Judea, but in saving souls.

Jeshua knew that the spirit of God could never be compromised, but the soul wasn't the same as the spirit. While the spirit was that part of God inside people that enabled them to have eternal life, it was the soul that projected their values, morality, intellects, personalities, hopes, and dreams; and which carried the memories of all of their deeds and misdeeds in their current life, as well as their past ones.

As Jeshua began to attract huge crowds whenever he spoke in Jerusalem, he became a concern for the Romans. They realized that his actions were independent of the Sanhedrin, that group of 70 elderly men appointed by the Jewish people to manage their religious affairs. In order to be a member of the Sanhedrin, which was a lifetime appointment, one had to be over 50 and the father of at least one son. The Romans held the Sanhedrin responsible for the behavior of the people and charged them with keeping the populace in line and making sure they didn't challenge Roman rules and demands.

The Sanhedrin was also responsible for the management of the temples, selecting which young men were to enter into the priesthood and which priests were assigned to the various temples. But in the case of Jeshua, the Romans realized that the Sanhedrin had no control or influence over his activities. And yet here was this man preaching almost daily on the temple grounds in front of huge crowds. And it was also rumored that he could perform magic, such as healing the sick, giving sight to the blind, and enabling the crippled to walk. Since this man didn't take instructions from the Sanhedrin, the Romans realized it was only a matter of time before they would have to take action on their own against him—before he became so powerful and popular that he could motivate the people to rebel.

The Last Supper

That was the atmosphere that existed on the first night of Passover in the city of Jerusalem. The Passover holiday was one of great joy for the Jews, for it celebrated the freeing of the Jewish people from slavery by the Egyptians in 1250 B.C., at the time of Moses. The first night of Passover was the most important one, and the same ceremonies were performed by Jewish people all over the world, as is also true today.

Jeshua and a number of his friends and pupils—not just 12 of them, but many more—met in the luxurious home of Zebedee in the Upper City for the feast and ceremonies. Zebedee was the father of disciples John and James and owned a fleet of fishing boats in the Sea of Galilee. It was to be Jeshua's "Last Supper."

Jeshua had been given the honor of sitting at the head of the table. A ritual is conducted in the ceremonies performed to this day in Jewish homes on the first night of Passover. The youngest person would be assigned the responsibility of chanting the Four Questions, which begin: *Dear Father, I wish to ask you four questions. The first question is, why is this day different from any other day?* . . . and so on. During the ceremony, the person at the seat of honor would take a large piece of unleavened bread, *matzo;* break off a small amount and put it in his or her mouth to eat; and pass the remainder for each person at the table to do the same. He would also take a sip of wine from a large goblet and pass it around, with each person taking a sip, also, when it was his or her turn.

Paul wasn't at the Last Supper, so I'm not in a position to tell you if indeed Jeshua said, "This bread is my body" as he held the matzo, and "This is my blood" as the goblet was passed around for each person to sip. Today, of course, Christians call this ceremony the *Eucharist,* and it is repeated in thousands of churches weekly throughout the world when people come forward to receive Communion—that is, taking a bite of a wafer and a sip of wine, symbolizing the body and blood of Jeshua. I have no issue with that ritual, but I find it interesting that at no time have I ever heard Christian representatives explain its background and its relationship to the Passover ceremony.

It is apparent that the 4th-century church leaders didn't want people to identify Jeshua as having been a Jew and acknowledge that he was actually celebrating his religion the day before he died. Instead, they have consistently tried to portray the Jewish people as being enemies of Jeshua and hostile to him, as you will discover in greater detail in the pages to follow.

Jeshua was arrested that evening after dinner as he and some of his followers were resting in a park in Jerusalem called Gethsemane, preparing to spend the night there. It was April, and the weather was pleasant and comfortable for sleeping outdoors. The scriptures say he was arrested by Herod's soldiers, but that isn't true. He was actually arrested by Roman soldiers.

Jeshua wasn't in hiding. He was preaching daily at the temple and could have been taken into custody at any time by the Romans. I assume they may have chosen to do so in the late evening, rather than during the day, because otherwise they might have attracted a large crowd around him who could have reacted violently as they tried to protect him.

The Devastating Lie

And now we come to one of the most detestable and criminal lies in the history of the world. The Gospels of Mark and Matthew tell us that in the middle of the night following the arrest of Jeshua—let us assume 3 or 4 in the morning—the Sanhedrin were convened and met at the council room, which was located in the southwestern corner of the temple grounds. The scriptures claim that Jeshua was brought before the Sanhedrin and was ordered to give them testimony, and as a result of that testimony, they demanded that Pontius Pilate have him killed that morning.

This story is a total fabrication made up by the early church leaders (who were controlled by the Roman government) to ensure that the Romans wouldn't be held responsible for the death of Jeshua.

Let's review in detail the gross absurdity of these false allegations that have persisted now for centuries. It was the holy night of Passover. The members of the Sanhedrin were asleep in their homes, scattered around Jerusalem, a city with a population of more than 400,000. There were no telephones, no iPhones, no Internet. Messengers would have had to visit the homes of each of the 70 elderly men, and for what? If they wanted to have a meeting, they could have done so the next morning—there was no urgency. The Romans were holding Jeshua in jail at the Antonia Fortress, located at the northwest corner of the temple grounds.

Does it make one iota of sense that they would wake up these 70 elderly Jewish men in the middle of the night for a trial of Jeshua, as described in the Gospels of Mark and Matthew? The Romans never consulted the Sanhedrin on these types of issues. And the Sanhedrin didn't utilize capital punishment. Only the Romans had the power to sentence someone to death. And *they* couldn't have cared less what the Jews did or did not want. The Romans were crucifying Jews every week in Jerusalem, as many as a dozen a month.

No, the Sanhedrin never met to condemn Jeshua. It was the Romans who brought him out of his jail cell the next day. It was then, in the presence of three members of the Sanhedrin summoned to attend the meeting, that Pilate accused Jeshua of preaching that there was somebody in Jerusalem more powerful than the emperor. The scriptures falsely claim that a crowd of Jewish people stood outside Pilate's quarters, shouting that he put Jeshua to death.

As I shared with you earlier, J and the angels (through Janet) both told the identical story: that it was Pilate, in a rage, who commanded his guards to replace Barabbas with Jeshua in the crucifixion that was to take place that morning at Golgotha.

But the Gospels state, as I mentioned in the last chapter, that Pilate poured water over his hands, and they have him yelling out: "I am innocent of this man's blood; see to it yourselves." To which the Jewish mob supposedly replied: "His blood be on us and on our children."

Consider, however, that we are talking about a man (Pilate) who crucified hundreds of Jews while he was in charge of the Holy Land for the Romans. Yet the Gospels have him stating he wanted nothing to do with the decision of the Jews to have Jeshua crucified.

It's hard to believe that there was an angry Jewish mob gathered outside of Pilate's quarters, yelling that they wanted Jeshua dead and that they wanted their children to be cursed over his death. Not only would a fictitious mob of Jewish people not have had access to Pilate, but the Roman representative wouldn't have cared what they had to say anyway. And the people worshipped

Jeshua. He preached love and truth to them daily at the temple and healed the sick. How could such ridiculous lies have survived 1,600 years, inciting prejudice and hate?

The Persecution

As the 4th-century scribes were translating the scriptures, Christian leaders made sure that the Romans would never be held responsible for the death of Jeshua. So who *could* they hold responsible?

The Jews were their logical choice, even though the Roman soldiers were the ones who beat Jeshua; nailed him to the cross; put mocking signs underneath him, calling him (in Latin) the King of the Jews; and placed a crown of thorns on his head to further ridicule him. *No matter,* these leaders reasoned, *blame it on the Jews.* They created a trial at 3 or 4 in the morning that never occurred; accused the Jews of condemning Jeshua to death; and contended that this meek, merciful man, Pontius Pilate, did not want to crucify Jeshua.

Now you understand why the church leaders tried to create a scenario to portray the Jewish people as being at odds with Jeshua, rather than revealing the love and respect they had for him. That is why they didn't even mention that the ritual of Passover was the basis for the Eucharist, and de-emphasized that Jeshua was celebrating a very holy Jewish holiday the night before the Romans killed him.

The horrific lies perpetrated by the Romans and Christianity's leaders have fomented a hatred toward the Jewish people resulting in the torture and murder of Jews for 2,000 years. These lies still continue today. This is what creates the anti-Semitism found in the twisted minds of certain ignorant individuals who claim the Holocaust never happened.

Let us look at the consequences that came about as a result of the actions of the 4th-century Christian leaders.

From A.D. 66 to 73, beginning some 33 years after Jeshua died, the Romans conducted a siege against Jerusalem, resulting in the starvation, burning, and slaughter of hundreds of thousands of Jews in that city. Sixty years later, the Romans again attacked the Holy Land, and it is estimated that they slaughtered hundreds of thousands more. They basically wiped out the population of Jews, including those who had accepted Jeshua as their Messiah. And in the next attack against the Jews in Jerusalem, in A.D. 135, the Romans killed or expelled the remaining Jewish people and renamed the city Syria Palaestina.

By the 4th century, the Roman Empire had become a Christian nation. Holding the Jewish people responsible for the killing of Jeshua in the scriptures had now become an impetus for cruelty by the Christian leaders against the Jews. For example, in A.D. 388, a Christian mob led by a bishop burned their temples and killed thousands in Callinicum and Milan.

In A.D. 414, the Jewish populations in Antioch were attacked and killed, and in Alexandria, the Jewish community was destroyed. Laws were passed denying Jews many rights; subjecting them to perpetual serfdom, including not being able to own land; and forbidding them from holding professional occupations.

In 1096, crusaders, at the urging of Pope Urban II, drove across northwestern Europe, killing every Jewish person they could find as they ravaged and pillaged the towns and villages they came across. During this Crusade, the first of seven, Pope Urban had promised the people rewards in their afterlives. Imagine the sight of a mob of thousands—made up of knights and their foot soldiers, servants, and peasants, along with the scum of the earth, who were let out of prisons and allowed to join them—with lances, swords, clubs, and knives. And while only some were wearing armor, they *all* were wearing the cross.

They gathered in northwestern Europe and drove through the Netherlands, France, Germany, and then on to Constantinople and Nicaea, sacking villages and raping women along the way. All in the name of God and Jeshua! Although most people generally associate the Crusades with an attempt to root out Islam, during the first two months of the summer of 1096, over 10,000 Jews were murdered, about a third of the Jewish population living in northern Europe.

It is recorded that in that year in the town of Worms, Germany, the local Jewish people asked the Christian leaders there to protect them from the oncoming crusaders. These leaders assured the Jews that they wouldn't be harmed and persuaded them to gather in their temple and lock themselves in for protection. When the crusaders arrived, they set fire to the temple and burned alive every one of the Jews inside.

All of the above happened as a result of the heinous lies of the Romans, perpetuated by the Christian leaders, blaming the Jewish people for the crucifixion of Jeshua, because the Romans themselves would not take responsibility.

In the 12th century, the hatred toward the Jews in Europe gave rise to the *blood libel*, the incredible accusation that Jews were killing young Christian boys as a reenactment of the crucifixion of Jeshua, which resulted in riots against the Jewish people. In France, they were burned alive at the stake on charges of poisoning wells. In 1347, when the plague hit Europe, the Jewish people again were accused of poisoning their wells, and more than 300 Jewish communities were destroyed.

The Fourth Lateran Council created by Pope Innocent III passed resolutions that isolated, denigrated, and restricted the Jewish people even further. They had to dress a certain way, remain hidden in their homes during Holy Week, and were subject to special taxation to be paid to the church.

The Spanish Inquisition came into being in the Middle Ages, and thousands of Jews were tortured. This information is so overwhelming that it is almost impossible to fathom.

Now let us come to more modern times, to bring home the incredible injustice that has been perpetrated against the Jewish people in the name of God. When Nazi Germany rounded up the Jews and imprisoned them in concentration camps, Pope Pius XII did not protest the Holocaust, and he supported the Nazis (even though the Catholic Church denies this). When more than 2,000

Italian Jews who lived just miles from the Vatican were arrested and sent to concentration camps, the Pope didn't say a word.

The Pope fought for protection from the Nazis for people who were handicapped or had mental disorders, urging that they be released from the concentration camps, but asked for no aid for the Jews. Germany was a Christian nation. Adolf Hitler was a Catholic, and when he came to power in 1933, the Vatican signed an accord with the Third Reich, representing a bilateral treaty with Hitler, the first foreign power to do so. Pope Pius and Hitler had made an agreement that the Catholic Church would not object to the führer's actions in return for his imposing a "church tax" on the people in Germany and Austria. That tax still exists today. Following the end of the war, Croatian priests were part of the infamous "rat lines," which helped the Nazis escape to South America, an operation that was conducted in Rome from a Vatican-affiliated Catholic college.

It is estimated that there are only 14 million Jews left on Earth today, half in Israel and half scattered across the globe. And even today, anti-Semitism runs rampant throughout the world. At what point is the Church going to acknowledge the sins they committed against these people and ask for forgiveness?

Pope Paul VI began that process, but his efforts have been reversed by the current Pope and those who control and administer the activities of the Church in the Vatican. Pope Benedict XVI has reinstated the Easter Latin Mass, which his predecessor had stopped, accusing the Jewish people of *deicide,* the killing of Jeshua. He has also reinstated Bishop Williamson, who had been removed from the Church by Pope Paul VI and who, among other things, preached that the Holocaust never happened.

My plea to the leaders of the Catholic Church is this: *the time for truth is now!* Forgiveness can be yours, but it can only come about if there is a reconciliation with God, a true expression of sorrow and remorse and acknowledgment of the incredible crimes committed against the Jewish people. I ask the Church: Do you have the courage to acknowledge the truth and ask for forgiveness? How do you think your actions look in the eyes of Jeshua and God?

I don't practice any religion. My relationship with God is a spiritual one, and does not take place within an organized institution. But I believe in the important role that religion can play in the world. As Spirit told me, it is not our intention to try to hurt the Church, but to do everything in our power to save it. It is not too late for the Church to be forgiven. Our God is a loving God, not a vengeful God.

Church leaders influence the lives of the 1.2 billion people who are members of the Catholic faith, as well as practitioners of other Christian religions who look to them for spiritual leadership. Do they have the courage to tell them the truth? Do they not understand that Jeshua and God *know* the truth? We are all God's children. No one can indiscriminately slaughter God's children without leaving a terrible mark on their souls. It is time for Church leaders to remove that mark, to be healed, to help heal the world, and to receive the forgiveness of God and Jeshua. When they have the integrity and spiritual strength to ask for atonement and redemption, only then can forgiveness be granted.

Chapter 16

The Apostle's Commitment

A day has gone by, and I've read and reread the words I wrote yesterday. And I now feel a very deep sadness within me—not for having written what I did, but because there was a *need* for me to do so.

In reality, this book isn't being composed exclusively by me, Nick Bunick. My name is not of any more importance than the clothes I'm wearing as I sit here before my computer. This book is being written by my spirit and soul, the same ones that manifested 2,000 years ago. But it is through my 2010 eyes and my 2010 intellect that I am able to see the consequences of my spirit and soul's activities when Paul traveled throughout the Roman Empire preaching, creating the basis for Christianity.

After the death of Jeshua, there was a great sadness that befell the people in the Holy Land who were his followers. Most were in shock and denial. They asked, *How could the life of this beautiful human being be taken, a person who only knew love and compassion and spoke the truth?*

Jeshua never uttered a word against the Romans, for he wasn't a political person. He was the messenger of God; and he wanted to teach people how to live their lives manifesting love, how to have a close personal relationship with God, and how to enjoy life and let others enjoy it through them. He taught that in a house with a master and a servant, we should never assume that the master has happiness and the servant is deprived of such, because happiness has nothing to do with wealth or status. He taught that happiness is generated by the love you give to others, for whatever you give is what you receive in return.

Paul was in mourning for a long period of time. He had great difficulty accepting that Jeshua was no longer on Earth. Paul became very reclusive and spent many hours in the mountains and hills outside of Jerusalem, in solitude and his own thoughts.

The Brotherhood

The Master was gone, and those he had taught were no longer his pupils. Instead, they were to become teachers of his words. The disciples would now be apostles (from the ancient Greek word *apostolos,* which means "teacher").

They formed their organization in Bethany, a short distance from Jerusalem, not far from the home of Mary Magdalene. Sometimes they referred to themselves as the Brotherhood, other times as the Witnesses. They organized themselves, appointing 70 people, just like the Sanhedrin, to become the leaders of their new organization.

These apostles developed rules that needed to be met in order for a person to become part of the Brotherhood. They required that the entire wealth of the individual or family be donated to the Brotherhood so that no one was wealthier than another, and everything was to be shared equally. This became a communal atmosphere that appealed to many people, particularly those who had been struggling economically. And for those who had been touched by Jeshua when he was alive, it gave them joy and peace to be able to live side by side, to be part of each other's lives.

Paul decided not to become part of their organization. It wasn't like him to be a member of a group, and he was very unhappy with some of the decisions the Brotherhood had made. They had begun to issue the threat that if people held any of their wealth back—rather than giving it to them—God would punish them. Paul believed that this was very wrong, and Jeshua would never have approved. He also felt that a large number of people were joining the group not because they identified with the teachings of Jeshua, but because they benefited from the sharing of material goods. They also made Peter their leader, and held up Jeshua's brother James as their figurehead leader. Paul didn't agree with those decisions.

It is written in the scriptures that Paul persecuted the apostles and their followers, and this isn't true. Paul was a businessman, not in any position that would give him the authority to persecute another. In fact, within the Judaic faith, people never persecuted other Jews because they didn't like the way they practiced their religion. There were a number of different sects of Judaism, including the Pharisees (of which Paul was one), the Sadducees, the Essenes, and other smaller groups.

No, there was no persecution by Paul or anybody else of that religion, but he did criticize some of the apostles' tactics that he didn't agree with. More than likely this accusation by the Christian church that Paul was persecuting the Brotherhood was an attempt to imply that he wasn't initially a believer in the teachings of Jeshua, which is not true.

Paul isn't mentioned in the four Gospels, for he wasn't considered a disciple and wasn't on friendly terms with those referred to as the 12 disciples. The relationship between Jeshua and the disciples was that of teacher and pupil, whereas Paul had a very intimate peer relationship with him, which they resented. As I mentioned before, most of the original 12 disciples were simple fishermen from Galilee who couldn't read or write, and Jeshua would speak to them in simple terms, which they still often didn't understand. On the other hand, Paul was educated, and his talks with Jeshua were at a different level.

As time went on, more and more people joined the Brotherhood. In Antioch, Jeshua's followers began to be called *Christians,* because it was believed that he was the Christ, one who had been anointed by God. This was a belief shared by Paul, and this name was also adopted by the Brotherhood.

The Road to Damascus

It had been five years since Jeshua's death, and Paul was spending a good deal of his time taking care of his business activities. It was in the fifth year that he decided to accept an invitation to go to Damascus to explore some opportunities there. It is falsely written in the scriptures that the purpose of his journey to Damascus was to arrest some Syrian Jewish citizens because he objected to their having accepted Jeshua as their Messiah, as the Brotherhood in Jerusalem had done. In other words, the scriptures ridiculously claim that Paul—a Jew in Jerusalem—traveled 140 miles across the desert to a foreign country because he didn't like the way they were practicing their religion there.

One would wonder how many of these Syrian Jews Paul was to arrest. Let's say it was to be five men. We're asked by religious leaders to believe that he would fight these five men single-handedly, and place them under his custody. And Paul would then be required to get them past the soldiers guarding the gates of Damascus. We're then supposed to believe that he would rent five camels, one for each of the prisoners tied or chained together, and then travel two weeks through the desert. He would have to stop at intervals to feed them and allow them to sleep at night, as well as to permit them to take care of their bodily functions. And once Paul arrived with his prisoners in Jerusalem, he would then presumably take them to the Romans and tell them he had arrested and kidnapped these five men, traveling through the desert with them so the Romans could punish them . . . for practicing their religion, as the Brotherhood was already doing in Jerusalem.

It's amazing that the leaders of the Christian church in the 4th century could make such absurd claims. If Paul were to enter

Damascus with such a mission, he would have either been immediately killed or locked up for life after being deemed insane.

No, that wasn't what happened. As I said, Paul had decided to travel to Damascus to explore a business opportunity with some Syrians. (This would have involved purchasing and subdividing land to be used by tenant farmers, as he had done in Judea.)

In the Holy Land at that time, there were convoys that you could hire to escort you from Jerusalem to Damascus and back. They would supply the camels and provide the food to eat and prepare it on the journey; and they were also trained to offer protection against possible thieves along the route.

There were four others who had also contracted to go to Syria on this same trip, although Paul didn't know them. Upon reaching the gates of Damascus, they had to pay a toll in order to gain entry. The gates were closed during the hours of darkness, and it was necessary to wait until sunrise to enter. Paul and his group arrived at night, so they stopped and made camp at Kakae, a small village with an oasis about ten miles outside of Damascus. It was there that Paul had his encounter with Jeshua.

It is preached and taught in the churches across the world today that this is when Paul had his "conversion." Yet I ask . . . conversion to what? The only nonpagan religion that existed was Judaism. Is the Christian church trying to imply that Paul at that time gave up his Jewish religion and converted to Christianity? It was Paul, five years later, who *founded* Christianity. So the leaders of the church had the scribes of the 4th century falsify the scriptures to claim that Paul had traveled to Damascus to arrest Jews in that city who had accepted Jeshua as the Messiah, and that along the way, he converted to Christianity, a religion that didn't exist. What was their intent, then, to have created this incredible false story, and what is their intent in perpetuating it today?

That is not what happened along the way to Damascus. Yes, when they camped in Kakae, Paul *did* have an extraordinary experience that changed his life. He awoke in the middle of the night and felt compelled to walk farther into the desert, away from the campsite. And he *did* have the experience of being with Jeshua, which was the most profound of his entire life. The light around Jeshua was so brilliant that it *did* temporarily affect his eyesight. (It is mentioned in the scriptures that upon seeing the light around Jeshua, Paul was temporarily blinded.)

But there was no conversion. What *did* take place was that Jeshua asked Paul to make a *commitment,* not a conversion: he asked him to commit to helping the apostles succeed in their mission, to assume responsibility as a leader, and to spread his messages to others throughout the world. And it was in the middle of that desert, on that starlit night outside of Damascus, that this businessman from Tarsus made his commitment to Jeshua to become the Apostle Paul, as he is known today.

The Apostle

After Paul returned from Damascus, he visited the Brotherhood headquarters in Bethany. He recounted the experience he'd had on the way to Damascus, and told them he was committed to helping them spread the messages of Jeshua. Although the members of the group had mixed emotions, for Paul had never been close to them when they were disciples, he was nevertheless accepted. He soon discovered that there wasn't much for him to do within the three provinces of Palaestina, for the group had been recruiting people for several years, so he made a decision to travel outside of the Holy Land to other countries within the Roman Empire.

It was then that he changed his name from Saul back to Paul. It was more important for him to have the protection of his Roman citizenship, as opposed to being identified as someone from Judea. He studied maps and made a list of the places he would travel to and the itinerary he would follow. He wasn't concerned about being able to communicate with the local people, for almost everyone spoke Greek in addition to their native language. This was a legacy from the time Alexander the Great and his armies had occupied the lands now controlled by the Romans. The Greeks had required the local people to learn their language, so this was the common way for foreigners to communicate with one another.

But Paul soon learned that only about 2 percent of the population in those countries outside of the Holy Land was Jewish. In some places, people were receptive to the news that he shared with them, and in others they weren't. But in every place he visited, he discovered that there was a very large number of people who weren't Jewish but had for years shown a great interest in becoming part of the religion. They didn't believe in the false idols of the Romans or think there was any benefit in praying to a lemon tree. They wanted to be part of the Jewish religion, but couldn't meet the three requirements to be accepted into it:

1. Men had to be circumcised.
2. People were required to totally change the food choices they were accustomed to and eat only "clean" food, as was agreed upon by the Jewish people and God in the covenant.
3. They must spend considerable time studying and learning the Jewish faith.

Any one of the three conditions was a great deterrent to Gentiles and pagans who might want to become members of the Jewish religion.

Many of these people pleaded with Paul to be allowed to learn and accept the teachings of Jeshua and the belief in one Divine being, our God, without having to meet the three requirements just mentioned. Paul felt this was a reasonable request. Wasn't it better for them to have Jeshua as their Savior, and God as their deity, than to be denied those gifts? Since they would never be allowed to practice these beliefs in a Jewish temple, why couldn't they have their own churches in which to do so?

Paul returned to Jerusalem after being gone for approximately three years. There were many heated debates over the next two years. Many insisted that only Jews could have Jeshua as their Messiah, but in the end, Paul's arguments won them over to his side. And now he was ready to begin his next mission, at the age of

46: he traveled to places such as Antioch; his birthplace of Tarsus; Derbe; Lystra; and then across the sea to Greece, to Athens and Corinth.

As Paul traveled throughout the Roman Empire, he preached to many thousands of people, opening churches in almost every city he visited. He selected those who had the skills and intelligence to be local leaders before he moved on. And I say to you that *many of his apostles and administrators were women.* He honored and respected these women and wrote of them in his letters, complimenting them and thanking them.

But early Christian leaders chose to deny that many of Paul's administrators and apostles were women. When he praised them in his letters in the scriptures, they changed their names to those of men. Years later when the Christian church was officially formed in the 4th century, women were denied the right to hold positions of responsibility. And the church leaders performed these acts claiming they were following Paul's doctrines, Paul's rules, and the regulations that Paul had established . . . and this is all false.

Lucius and Celibacy

One man Paul appointed to a position of responsibility was his dear friend Lucius. He placed him in charge of his churches in Laodicea, for he knew the man had the leadership qualities and the intelligence to handle these duties. But Lucius became a major embarrassment to Paul when he got involved in a relationship with a local married woman, a Roman by the name of Vesta. Lucius was married to a Jew, Mariah, when Vesta gave birth to his child. This was a terrible scandal, and Paul had no choice but to remove Lucius from his position.

After much thought, Paul made a decision, in the hopes that an incident like that would never again happen. He declared that from that time on his administrators had to maintain marital fidelity. It was unacceptable for any of them to involve themselves sexually with another person outside of marriage. If a church administrator felt the need to be intimately involved with someone,

Paul told the person that he or she should marry. In other words, unmarried ministers should not get in relationships with the local people and should be wed if they felt a need to do so.

At no time did Paul ever declare that his ministers had to be unmarried men and remain celibate. But again, his words were twisted, as the 4th-century religious leaders adopted a regulation that they claimed was attributed to Paul, stating that only men could hold positions of leadership, but they must remain single and celibate. This was wrong. What right did they have to deny married men and women entry into the priesthood?

They were no doubt concerned that when priests died, they would leave their estates to their children, rather than to the church; and reasoned that by not allowing them to marry, there would be no heirs. Paul never would have condoned such actions—there is no excuse for these distortions of the truth.

There's an extremely interesting and important story that I feel must be shared with you at this time.

After the publication of *The Messengers*, I was invited to be a guest at the headquarters of the Edgar Cayce Foundation. If you're not familiar with Edgar Cayce, he was the greatest seer who ever lived. Cayce could put himself into a trance, and while in that state, he was omniscient. He was able to tap into universal knowledge. He knew the past, present, and future of all that exists. He could even diagnose the illness of a person thousands of miles away, describing the sickness, its cause, and its cure. He did this hundreds of times. He could also tell people about their past lives. Thousands of readings that he gave when he was in his trance state were recorded, and many books have been written about his extraordinary gift.

When I arrived at the campus of the Edgar Cayce headquarters in Virginia Beach, Virginia, I was treated with great hospitality. I had an interview with the foundation's magazine editor, which was featured over five pages in their publication the following month. The next morning I enjoyed breakfast at the home of

Cayce's grandson, a man then in his 60s, who shared stories of his grandfather with me.

But the extraordinary part of this story was that I was shown that in a reading Cayce had given many years before, he identified himself as having been Lucius almost 2,000 years earlier. He also described the exact events I've just told you of: being married to Mariah; having an affair and a child with the married Roman woman, Vesta; and then being relieved of his position by Paul.

The two experiences—Edgar Cayce telling this story while in a trance and my also describing these same details while under hypnosis through the memory of Paul—*are* an extraordinary confirmation of this incident in history. This was the one that the Christian leaders in the 4th century would use as an excuse to falsely claim that Paul had demanded that priests be unmarried, as well as celibate.

In the next chapter you will learn how the Roman Catholic Church came to be. It's a story that is rarely discussed and isn't taught in churches. Hold on to your hat as we continue on our journey.

Chapter 17

The Birth of the Roman Catholic Church

In A.D. 312, the most powerful person in the world stood on the Milvian Bridge, ready to take his army into battle. His name was Constantine, and he was the emperor of a Roman territory that stretched all the way across Europe, included the Byzantine land on its eastern border, and controlled more than 80 million people. Never before had there been an empire as large and powerful, covering such a huge distance.

Constantine stood on this bridge surrounded by his most capable soldiers, men committed to protecting him on the battlefield. He was concerned about the outcome because his enemy outnumbered him, and he looked to the skies for a sign from his gods. What Constantine claimed he saw—an image of a cross—would change the world forever. He believed it inspired him and his army to be victorious in this important battle.

Following his victory, Constantine and his advisors announced to the world that from that day on, Rome would no longer be pagan, but instead would accept the concept of one God, the Christian God. He declared that the cross thereafter would be the symbol of their acceptance of Christ, and universal Christianity would become the religion of the Roman Empire.

At that time there were a number of different versions of Christianity being practiced. Constantine and his advisors chose one to continue at the expense of the others. The properties belonging to the rival Christian sects' churches were to be given to the one selected by Constantine, which had confined its scriptures to the four Gospels and espoused a belief that only the leaders of the church should be authorized to interpret these writings. And thus was created the Roman Universal Church.

Shortly thereafter, in A.D. 325, the new church held its first ecumenical Council of Nicaea. Nicaea was a wealthy community about 20 miles south of the city of Constantinople. Many decisions were made at that council's meetings that would change the world, perhaps making this time in history the period that had the greatest impact on the future. The changes in the teachings of Jeshua and Paul were so drastic, so profound, that had they not been made, the history of humankind over the last 1,600 years would have been totally different, and we would be living in a different world today.

The Gospels were first written in Aramaic, a language that originated in Chaldea, an ancient Asian country located on the Euphrates River. There was a great similarity between Aramaic and Hebrew. Like Hebrew, the words ran from right to left; and there was no punctuation, no demarcation of sentences, no paragraphs. To the reader, a scroll of six pages would appear as one continuous word six pages long.

From that language, the Gospels were then translated into Greek. It was a tremendous challenge to undertake, for oftentimes the scribes had to guess where a sentence ended and what meaning was intended. Another translation took place during the formation of the Christian church by the Roman Empire, in which the Gospels were translated from Greek to Latin. It is important to understand that if an error was made by a scribe, it became a permanent change in the scriptures. All these writings were laboriously reproduced, each new scroll a supposed true copy of the one before it.

The first Council of Nicaea took place in A.D. 325, and it was in A.D. 382 that a group of scribes was commissioned to translate the scriptures from Latin to what was considered at that time the modern-day written language of the Romans. Not only did errors continue to occur inadvertently, but it was also the deliberate intention of the Christian leaders to change many of the events that took place in the Gospels to serve their own purposes. It took the scribes 23 years to complete the translations, which resulted in the official Bible for Western Christendom from that day on.

Many words got changed during these translations, even if those changes weren't intentional, such as the original Aramaic word *naggar,* which could either refer to a scholar, an educated man, or a craftsman. Visualize the scribe sitting on his stool, with his scroll placed on a slanted wooden desk, pondering the intended meaning of the original word. Was Jeshua a scholar or a craftsman? For whatever reason, that translator made the decision to treat the word as having meant the latter, and that is why we are erroneously told today, 1,600 years later, that Jeshua's profession was that of a carpenter.

This was not an earthshaking error, but a more significant one may have occurred in describing his mother, Mary. The early scriptures refer to her as an *almah* when she gave birth to Jeshua. *Almah* could either mean a young girl or a virgin, as I mentioned in the last chapter, since the assumption was that a young girl was most likely a virgin. Mary was only 16 when she gave birth to Jeshua. Was she a young girl who was *also* a virgin?

This interpretation was tremendously controversial to the populace at the time it was put forward. From my perspective, a change that may or may not have occurred in translating *almah* doesn't change who Jeshua and Mary were, or their role in history. But it is indicative of many of the alterations that arose from human error.

The Translations

Two thousand years ago most of the people of the Roman Empire were illiterate. It's estimated that only about 10 percent of the populace was capable of reading and writing. It is even stated in Acts 4:13 that Peter and John were illiterate. But the written word did play an important role in the growth of religion. It was not uncommon for a scribe to read from scrolls to others who couldn't read, and then the stories would get repeated over and over again orally, by rote. But obviously, if the original reading wasn't accurate, the story carried on from that day forth would also be inaccurate.

The study of the manuscripts of the New Testament is known as "textual criticism." Bart D. Ehrman is one of the foremost experts in this area. He initially studied at Moody Biblical Institute and then attended Wheaton College, where he developed an expertise on the scriptures in both Greek and Hebrew. He continued his impressive academic career at Princeton Theological Seminary.

This outstanding scholar researched the New Testament, not with the intent to challenge the motives of Christianity or its scholars, but rather to provide an objective analysis of the many changes that had been made. These modifications included the deletion of portions of the original writings, the changing of words and facts, as well as the addition of material that wasn't found in earlier versions of the same scriptures. Most of the information I'm sharing with you in this chapter came from the extensive professional work done by this scholar.

As for the New Testament, some 13 letters written in Paul's name are included in that text. But Paul wrote many more letters than just those 13. For example, in his First Epistle to the Corinthians, he mentions other correspondence he had written to them earlier, which is lost and has never been published. Other Gospels that aren't included in the New Testament are those by Philip, Thomas, and Mary Magdalene.

In A.D. 367 Athanasius was a powerful bishop in Alexandria. He listed 27 books he felt should be included in the New Testament, which caused a debate that lasted for decades. The books that make up what we now call the New Testament were finally selected as the only ones to be acknowledged, an event that came about hundreds of years after they had actually been written.

The scrolls had to be copied by hand, one at a time, and it was a painstaking and difficult process. One of the problems with the ancient texts, as I mentioned earlier, is that there were no marks of punctuation used, no distinction between upper- and lowercase letters, and no spaces to separate words. From the first word to the last, there was one continuous flow of letters. This created a tremendous opportunity for errors to be made by the scribes, and once one was made, it remained with every copy of that scripture from that day on, including those of today.

A perfect example is the Gospels' repeated claim that Paul persecuted the early founders of Christianity, which is totally false. The word should have been *criticized,* not *persecuted.* And Paul had reason to criticize them, which I discussed earlier.

In fact, the great Christian leader Origen made the following complaint:

> The differences among the manuscripts have become great, either through the negligence of some copyists or through the perverse audacity of others; they either neglect to check over what they have transcribed, or, in the process of checking, they make additions or deletions as they please.

It was a common practice for church leaders to have the scribes make changes in the texts of the scriptures to have them represent their own views. In fact, Marcion, one of the translators, was said to have had . . .

> . . . dismembered the epistles of Paul, removing all that is said by the apostle respecting that God who made the world, to the effect that He is the Father of our Lord Jesus Christ, and also those passages from the prophetical writings which the apostle quoted, in order to teach us that they announced beforehand the coming of the Lord . . .

As previously stated, once a change was made, either by error or intentionally, it became a permanent part of the scriptures.

In the Gospel of John, there is the story of an adulteress whom Jeshua stopped the people from stoning with the famous words: "He that is without sin among you, let him first cast a stone at her." It has been taught that this woman was supposed to be Mary Magdalene. Not only was Mary Magdalene not an adulteress, but this story *only* appears in the book of John, not in the other three Gospels. But in the original Aramaic copies of John, it does *not* appear. In other words, this is a false story that was later added to John's gospel by a scribe, yet it's still taught in churches around the world today.

In the last 12 verses of the Gospel of Mark, we are told that after Jeshua is crucified, he appears to Mary Magdalene and meets with the disciples, breaks bread with them, gives them instructions, and then ascends to heaven. I have no reservations accepting that Jeshua was resurrected, but those last 12 verses are absent from the two oldest and best copies of Mark's Gospel. In other words, they were added several hundred years after it was originally written.

It was in the 4th century that the scholars were hired by the Christian church to translate the scriptures from older Latin into a version known as the Vulgate. The scriptures had gone from Aramaic to Greek to Latin and now to Latin Vulgate. Prior to that translation, there were four kinds of manuscripts:

1. The oldest were **papyrus** manuscripts, written on material made from papyrus reed.

2. Then there was the **majuscule**, manuscripts with very large letters written on parchments from animal skins.

3. Next came the **minuscule**, which were small-lettered manuscripts, also on parchment.

4. Last were **lectionaries**, which contained portions of the scriptures rather than the whole books.

I share this with you so you can understand the different methods by which the scriptures were copied, and how one change, whether by error or intentionally, created a new version from that day on. Keep in mind that it was not until the 1400s that the printing press was invented.

Women and the Scriptures

There was a deliberate effort by the leaders of the Christian religion to eliminate the importance of women in the life of Jeshua, as well as their roles with respect to Paul. In all of Paul's letters, he would thank the people he had appointed in their respective churches, and many of them were women. Paul mentions Phoebe, whom he had appointed as minister in his church at Cenchreae; his ministers Prisca and Mary, who worked with the Romans; and Tryphena, Tryphosa, and Persis, whom Paul called his co-workers. And also mentioned were Julia, the mother of Rufus, and the sister of Nereus—all of whom Paul gave positions of responsibility to.

The above is very important to me personally. As I traveled around the country giving presentations, female members of the audience often came up to me to tell me they were surprised that I was so complimentary to women, for Christianity had painted a picture of Paul for the last 1,600 years as a man who discriminated against them.

I don't want to belabor this point, but let me be very specific. In the older versions of Romans 16, Paul calls a woman by the name of Junia one of his foremost apostles. In later copies of this passage, Junia's name was changed to a man's, calling "him" Junias. Also, in Acts, it was originally stated that among those who joined Paul were a very large number of prominent women, but it was later changed to read that they were the wives of prominent men.

In addition to not allowing priests to marry, religious leaders in the 4th century were committed to excluding women from holding positions in the priesthood, which they also blamed on Paul. And it is all untrue. That was not what happened, as I explained in the previous chapter, discussing what really took place 2,000 years ago.

But the saddest part is that the Vatican knows all of this. Catholic leaders know the truth, even if they deny it, which they probably will. Located in the Vatican is a secret vault where the ancient books are kept, and they're never made available to outsiders. They even officially call it the Vatican Secret Archives. There are hundreds of manuscripts and scrolls and parchments going back to the time of Jeshua when the Gospels were originally written.

But the Catholic Church won't give scholars access to these writings. The Vatican claims the oldest copy of the scriptures it has today was written around the 6th century, which is illogical. We have the writings of the famous Greek philosophers, like Socrates, Plato, and Aristotle; works such as *The Iliad* and *The Odyssey;* and other material that goes back hundreds of years before Jeshua was born. So why would the Church not have the earlier versions of the scriptures in the secret archives? Logic dictates that they do, and it's time for the Church to share the truth with the world!

In the next chapter, I want to share with you the historical background on reincarnation and the efforts by the Church to deny its truth.

Chapter 18

The Truth about Reincarnation

One of the most devastating changes that was made in the scriptures was a result of the Catholic Church's insistence that everything be purged out of the Gospels that referenced reincarnation. Leaders felt that only the church could be the conduit between the people and God, and that it alone was the route to salvation and redemption. But in these efforts to purge reincarnation from the scriptures, it was missed in two places: the Gospels of Matthew and John.

The Gospel of Matthew

In the last paragraph of the last chapter of the Old Testament, Malachi 4:5–6, it is prophesied that the prophet Elijah, also known as Elias, would be reborn again with the coming of the Messiah.

In Matthew 16:13–15, Jeshua meets some of his disciples in upper Galilee and asks them who people are saying they think he is. And they answer that some think he is the reincarnation of the prophet Elias. And Jeshua answers in Matthew 17:9–13 that he who was the reincarnation of Elias had already come and they had taken his life, and the disciples acknowledge that he is referring to John the Baptist.

One day in 1997, following the publication of *The Messengers*, I was doing a talk show with the host of a large radio station in Seattle. A caller by the name of David was insisting to me that there was no such thing as reincarnation, so I directed him to the Gospel of Matthew.

He responded by again telling me I was wrong, for I was misinterpreting that passage. So I asked him, "If the New Testament says that John the Baptist had been the prophet Elijah 900 years earlier, does that mean that when his mother, Elizabeth, gave birth to him, a 55-year-old man weighing 150 pounds came out of her womb?"

David snickered and said, "Of course not. Don't you see, it was the spirit of Elijah that was born from her womb."

And I answered, "But, David, you just described reincarnation."

There was about ten seconds of silence. Then I could hear the click of the phone as David hung up. Why? Because there is no explanation for that passage other than that Jeshua believed in reincarnation.

I was once at a function where I was conversing with a Catholic priest who didn't know my background. I casually mentioned that passage of Matthew and asked, "Doesn't that mean that Jesus believed in reincarnation?" He stared at me incredulously for a few seconds and then said I must be misunderstanding what the passage meant, and he got up and walked away.

There is no room for misinterpretation.

The Gospel of John

The other area that wasn't purged from the scriptures was John 9:1–4. Jeshua had just finished doing healings near a well in the marketplace in Jerusalem, and he and the disciples were leaving the area. A blind man was standing in the street, and one of the disciples asked Jeshua how it could be possible that this man was born blind—was it because of his previous sins or those of his parents? And Jeshua answered, "No, he was born blind to show the glory of God," and proceeded to heal him.

But the important point is that the man couldn't have been born blind from previous sins if he hadn't lived a previous *life*. I have noticed in some editions of the Bible that the wording has been changed to confuse what was being asked.

The changing of the wording in some of the editions of the scriptures to confuse the reader is not uncommon. In Paul's letter to the Romans, he wrote the following in Chapter 7:

> I did not know sin except through the law, and I did not know what it is to covet. . . . But sin, finding an opportunity in the commandment, produced in me every kind of covetousness, apart from the law. Sin is dead. I once lived outside the law, then I died, but when the commandments came, sin became alive, and the commandment that was for life turned out to be death for me.

What Paul was saying was that he lived prior to Moses bringing the Ten Commandments into law, and when he coveted at that time, he was outside of the law because the law didn't exist, and therefore what he did wasn't a sin. But when the commandments came into being, he had already died, and thus the sin only "became alive" when he was reborn in his present lifetime as Paul, as his coveting would now constitute a violation of the commandment. But the words in this passage of Paul's letter have often been intentionally rewritten to confuse readers, and in some editions the location in the paragraph where Paul said he died has been changed to make it seem as if he was referring to his death in his present lifetime. In that way, it wouldn't appear that he was stating he had lived prior to Moses.

At the time of Jeshua, the Jewish religion was made up of two main sects—the Pharisees and the Sadducees—and several smaller ones, one being the Essenes. The Sadducees were connected to the priests and temples and numbered fewer than the largest sect, the Pharisees. The Sadducees took the same position as the majority of the Jewish people today, in that they didn't claim to know what happened upon death. They believed that only God knew, whereas the Pharisees totally believed in reincarnation. Today's Hasidic Jews, recognizable for their black wardrobes and curled hair along their ears, still believe in reincarnation. But to the Jewish people 2,000 years ago, there was only one religion and one God; and they prayed in the same temples, rather than separating based on the belief systems of the different sects.

The History of Reincarnation

Reincarnation didn't begin with the Jews in Israel 2,000 years ago. Many people assume that today this belief is mostly confined to those who would be considered New Age thinkers. But the truth is that God created a foolproof system enabling souls to be reborn in order to continue to learn and discover the truth, and to eventually reach perfection and become at one with God and Christ Consciousness by consistently exercising universal compassion and love. And some of the greatest minds that have ever lived have understood this:

— **Pythagoras** (ca. 580–ca. 500 B.C.), a famous Greek philosopher, not only believed in reincarnation, but claimed that he had received as a gift from God the memory of his soul's past lives. He claimed that he had previously been Aethalides, who was then reborn as Euphorbus.

— **Aristotle** (384–322 B.C.) and his teacher, **Plato** (ca. 428–348 B.C.), are two of the greatest philosophers in history, and both believed in reincarnation. They stated in a number of writings that the soul of man is immortal and can perform its proper functions by continuing to reincarnate into different physical bodies at different times.

— The great writer and philosopher **Cicero** (106–43 B.C.), just years before Jeshua was born, stated that there is "strong proof of men knowing most things before birth, and when they are children, they grasp innumerable facts with such speed as to show that they aren't experiencing them for the first time, but remember them" from past lives. Don't we even see that occurring today when we discover a young child who can play concert piano despite never having had a lesson, or who paints as a great artist would?

— The famed Roman poet **Virgil** (70–19 B.C.) stated that all souls, after they have passed away, are summoned by the Divine once again. In this way they become forgetful of their former Earth lives as they return to their new living bodies.

— And last, **Plutarch** (A.D. 46–after 119), another great Greek scholar and philosopher, stated that every soul is ordained to wander between incarnations in the spiritual world until driven down again to Earth and coupled with a newborn baby's body.

So, as you can see, it was not unusual for the Jewish people at the time of Jeshua and Paul, who had exposure to the teachings of these great minds, to have also incorporated these truths into their beliefs. In fact, in the 1600s, Rabbi Manasseh ben Israel, a great Jewish scholar, stated in his book *Nismat Hayyim:*

> The belief or the doctrine of the transmigration of souls is a firm and infallible dogma accepted by the whole assemblage of our church with one accord, so that there is no one to be found who would dare to deny it. . . . Indeed, there are a great number of sages in Israel who hold firm to this doctrine so that they made it a dogma, a fundamental point of our religion. We are therefore in duty bound to obey and accept this dogma with acclimation, as the truth of it has been incontestably demonstrated by the Zohar, and all books of the Kabala.

According to the *Universal Jewish Encyclopedia,* reincarnation is a universal belief in Hasidism. In the encyclopedia, it answers the questions of what happens when a person dies young. It is stated:

> No human life goes to waste. If one of us dies before his time, his soul returns to earth to complete his span, to do the things left undone and experience the happiness and grief he would have known.

Compare this truth with the Vatican teaching that when an unbaptized baby dies, it goes to purgatory. And since it has only one life, according to the Church, how can it ever evolve and mature to have a true relationship with God? The child would never have any experiences or have an opportunity to learn right from wrong and make itself worthy of being with God.

The Jewish encyclopedia continues:

> It's not only the poor it pays to be careful with. You can't say for a certainty who any person might have been in their last existence, nor what they are doing on earth (now). Through many transmigrations, the human soul is drawn by pain and grief, as a child to his mother's breast, to the source of its being.

Josephus was a brilliant Jewish historian who was so respected by the Romans that after attacking the rebelling Israelis around A.D. 60, they brought him back to Rome and made him the official historian for the empire. Josephus wrote in his *The Antiquities of the Jews* (Book 18, Chapter 1, Number 2) that of the three sects of the Jews, the Sadducees didn't know whether the soul lived after death, but the Essenes and Pharisees believed that it did. He wrote: "The Pharisees believe that their souls have an immortal vigor in them and that the virtuous shall have the power to revive and live again."

He also stated in his address to the Jewish soldiers, found in *The Jewish War* (Book 3, Chapter 8, Number 5):

> The bodies of men are indeed mortal and created out of corruptible matter; but the soul is ever immortal. . . . Do ye not remember that all pure spirits when they depart out of this life obtain a most holy place in heaven, and they are then again sent into pure bodies . . . ?

Philo Judaeus was a famous 1st-century Jewish scholar from Alexandria. He wrote: "The air is full of souls; those who are nearest to earth descending to be tied to mortal bodies return to other bodies, designed to live in them."

Many of the early Christian leaders were totally supportive of their religion encompassing reincarnation. In the 2nd century, one of the most prominent such leaders was Justin Martyr, who spoke of the soul inhabiting more than one human body and said that as it took on new ones, it couldn't remember its previous experiences.

Gregory, who was eventually made a saint, lived in the 4th century and was the bishop of Nyssa. He wrote: "It is absolutely necessary that the soul shall be healed and purified, and if this does not take place during this life on earth, it must be accomplished in future lives."

Origen, who lived in the 3rd century, had a tremendous following and was the most prominent of all Christian fathers, with the exception of Augustine, whom I'll discuss in the next chapter. Origen was sometimes referred to as the greatest teacher of the early Greek church. He wrote:

> . . . is it not more in conformity with reason that every soul for certain mysterious reasons, as according to the opinion of Pythagoras and Plato and Empedocles, is introduced into a body and introduced according to its deserts and former actions? . . . Is it not rational that souls shall be introduced into bodies, in accordance with their merits and previous deeds, and those who have used their bodies in doing the most good shall have a right to bodies with qualities superior to the bodies of others?

I suspect that in translating Origen's words, the scribe should have used the word *lives* rather than *bodies* in several places, but the message is obvious.

Origen continued in his writings:

> Every soul . . . comes into this world strengthened by the victories or weakened by the defeats of its previous life. . . . Its work in this world determines its place in the world which is to follow this.

So just as the majority of the Jewish people in the three provinces believed in reincarnation at the time of Jeshua, so did most of the early Christian leaders and their followers in the non-Jewish Roman Empire after his death. This was to become a major problem in the first several hundred years of Christianity after Constantine and his subordinates formed the Roman Catholic Church. It's also important to note that the Roman leaders had tremendous control over the Church for the first approximately thousand years of its existence, in addition to selecting and appointing the Popes.

You might ask why I'm making such a concerted effort to have you accept the truth that you are not a human being who by coincidence has a spirit and soul, but are a spirit with a soul who is having a human experience. You may have been taught since you were a little child that you will have only one lifetime, that your relationship with God can only come through your religion, and that salvation and redemption can only occur through its intercessions. This has probably been drummed into you time and time again until you may even have been frightened to think differently, afraid that to do so would be a sin, and you would be punished by God. I can't begin to count the number of times people have approached me after one of my talks and told me that they had asked a church official a question about some of these issues, and the person got angry and told them to never ask again.

It is crucial that I give you every opportunity to understand the truth, no matter how repetitive it may appear, and no matter how many different ways I have to approach it. I am committed to helping you understand your relationship with God and your purpose in life: to become at one with God.

The Council of Constantinople

It was absolutely critical to early Christian leaders that their followers not believe in reincarnation. How could they control the lives of their parishioners if these individuals didn't believe they were all dependent on the church in order to have that special relationship with God? It was vitally important to these leaders that reincarnation be erased from all religious teachings and that Jeshua and Paul, who completely accepted reincarnation, be separated from that belief for all time.

So a major decision was made in A.D. 553, approximately 200 years after the Council of Nicaea, one that would have an impact on the world from that time on. During this period, the emperor was Justinian, a man of great power and achievement in the Roman Empire. He decided to declare war on the followers of Origen and the continued belief in reincarnation.

He called together the fifth ecumenical Council of Constantinople. With the exception of six bishops from Africa, its hearings were attended entirely by delegates from the eastern portion of the Roman Empire. Of the 165 who attended, 159 were from the Eastern church and were controlled by Justinian, who had refused Pope Vigilius's request for equal representation of the bishops from both East and West. No representatives from Rome were allowed to be present, for they didn't agree with what was about to occur. Pope Vigilius, who had been summoned to Constantinople, refused to attend, so the council was presided over by Eutychius, the patriarch of Constantinople and head of the Eastern church.

The council began on May 5, 553, and concluded its work by June 2. In less than one month, it passed 15 resolutions, called *anathemas*. An anathema meant that there would be a curse on those who did not accept and follow these new rulings.

The first anathema that passed stipulated that if anybody continued to teach and practice reincarnation, he or she would be excommunicated from the church. Also included was additional language warning of damnation to any inquiring mind who considered embracing these forbidden beliefs.

The language read:

> If anyone does not anathematize Arius, Eunomius, Macedonius, Apollinaris, Nestorius, Eutyches and Origen, as well as their impious writings, as also all other heretics already condemned and anathematized by the Holy Catholic and Apostolic Church, and by the aforesaid four Holy Synods and [if anyone does not

> equally anathematize] all those who have held and hold or who in their impiety persist in holding to the end the same opinion as those heretics just mentioned: let him be anathema.

The men mentioned were leaders who had written extensively about reincarnation being a part of Christianity. What the council basically accomplished through these actions was to declare that anybody who continued to believe in reincarnation would be cursed for eternity.

As a result of the decision to deny people the right to believe in reincarnation in the 6th century, and the continued denial today of the truth regarding the teachings of Jeshua and Paul (which included reincarnation), religion has fundamentally impacted *your* relationship with God, making it substantially different than it otherwise would be. There's a tremendous difference between recognizing and experiencing that you are part of God, God is part of you, and God's spirit resides within you . . . and having a third party insist that *it* is the conduit between you and God.

In the next chapter, I want to discuss religious leaders' obsession with making their followers believe that they are all sinners who need the church to save them from hell.

Chapter 19

CREATING HELL AND SINNERS

One of the most important challenges that early Christian leaders were confronted with was how they would be able to control the lives of the people. It was decided that in addition to creating fear in their followers, they would incorporate into their religious teachings and doctrines the notion that we are *all* sinners, and that atonement and redemption could only be received through the church.

Augustine

During the latter part of the 4th century, one of the most prominent leaders of the Christian faith was Augustine. He was so widely respected that he was eventually made a saint. Augustine came up with a brilliant idea that was actually very simple: have Christian doctrine claim that from the moment every child leaves its mother's womb, it is condemned by God to go to hell when it dies.

His colleagues responded, "How are you going to convince the Roman populace that a child, a newborn infant, is condemned by God to go to hell?"

"No problem," answered Augustine. "We will tell them it's because Adam took a bite out of the forbidden apple. Therefore, since we are all descendants of Adam, every newborn is condemned to go to hell because of that original sin."

This caused tremendous controversy among the Romans who had accepted Christianity. Many of them felt that it was ridiculous to believe that a child born of its mother's womb could be considered a sinner and be damned to hell. The arguments both for and against original sin were very intense.

It took Augustine 20 years to convince his colleagues to adopt the concept of original sin. This was very important, because then the church could perform a ceremony—*baptism*—on the newborn, which would provide the baby with redemption. The baby would have to become a member of the church, and the family would pay a fee . . . and then the child would not be condemned to go to hell, having now received salvation.

But even the Romans who allowed themselves to be baptized had a few concerns. Some of the adults were still fairly young people. They had a whole lot of sinning left to do in their lives. They worried that if the church gave them a ceremony now that redeemed them, what would happen when they died 20 or 30 years later and had sinned some more? Wouldn't they still end up in hell?

But the church leaders came up with another brilliant idea. On their deathbed, people would undergo another ceremony—*last rites*—that would reinstate their redemption and salvation so that they could gain entry into heaven.

Thus, as a result of Augustine's brilliant idea, were the practices of baptism and last rites adopted. What is even more incredible than the way in which the concept of original sin came about is the fact that this is still being taught today, more than 1,600 years later!

So for those people who don't receive these rites, the position of the religious authorities is that they will be punished by God and go to hell when they die. How is it possible to have universal love and compassion when one of the major world religions condemns others to hell—a place that *it* created—for not having the same beliefs? Does anyone actually think that this was the message that Jeshua was trying to convey? Are we truly to believe that we must accept a ceremony from the church to receive salvation because a snake persuaded a woman to convince her husband to bite into a forbidden apple?

Hell

Two thousand years ago, most people believed that the sky had a huge blue plate above it and heaven was beyond that plate. That's why they spoke of angels ascending or descending between Earth and the celestial realm, since heaven was above the sky, on the other side of the plate. And the stars at night were holes on the bottom of the plate, allowing the light in heaven to shine through.

Two thousand years ago, the area southwest of the walls of Jerusalem was known as the Valley of Hinnom. Here the people of Jerusalem created a dump where the population of more than 400,000 had their garbage delivered, and it burned 24 hours a day. This dump was called Gehenna. If a mother got angry at her child, she would threaten to send the child to Gehenna as punishment. And the English translation of the Hebrew word *Gehenna* is "hell." That is where Christianity got the concept of hell. If heaven is above the sky, then hell must surely be below the earth.

The early leaders of the church *needed* this hell that they created. It was the place they could use to frighten those who didn't abide by their rules and regulations: if people didn't believe in what their religion was preaching, God would punish them and they'd go to hell. How many people over the last two millennia have been threatened and "damned" to the hell that these leaders created? How many children's minds have been damaged by the threat of God's punishment in the afterlife?

A few months after *The Messengers* was released, I was giving a talk in the sanctuary of the beautiful headquarters of the Unity Church in Missouri. When I was through with my presentation, which lasted three hours, I stepped off the stage to do signings for those who had brought a copy of the book with them. At one point a handsome young man in glasses, wearing slacks and a sport shirt, stood before me with tears streaming down his face. He told me he was a Catholic priest, and he knew everything I had said that day to be true and didn't know what to do. He also told me that if I looked in the *Catholic Bible Dictionary,* I would find that the definition of *Gehenna* was "hell," as I had described based on my past-life memory while under hypnotic regression. I told him to continue teaching what he knew was the truth, and not what he didn't believe in, as there are many good things the Catholic Church does for those in need, as well as many benefits to communal worship, in spite of the mistruths that are preached.

When I got home the next day, I did look in my Catholic Bible, which contains a dictionary, and as the young priest had told me, *Gehenna* is defined as "hell."

On the cover of the January 31, 2000, edition of *U.S. News & World Report,* there was a picture of the devil smiling with a cocktail in his hand; behind him a man and woman in bathing suits lounged in chairs on a slab of rock, with fire on all sides of them. The headline read: "Hell: A New Vision of the Netherworld."

Inside the issue was a five-page article citing a poll stating that 64 percent of the people who had been asked believed in hell. In the article, Pope John Paul II was quoted as telling an audience at the Vatican that hell indicates the state of mind of "those who freely and definitively separate themselves from God." In other words, hell is not a *place,* but a state of being in which people suffer from the deprivation of God in their lives.

The article stated that the conservative critics at the Vatican complained that by dousing hell's flames, the Pope had undermined a historical biblical weapon in the Catholic Church's struggle against evil. Of course, the Pope was trying to bring the Church into the 21st century, but it's obvious that those who actually manage and control the affairs of the Vatican were successful in refuting his position and have kept the Church mired in its medieval beliefs. And after all, without a hell, where is the devil, another creation of Christianity, going to call home?

If indeed this fabrication of the church were actually true, this would mean that our God is a punishing God, and a sinful person upon death is consigned to eternal damnation without ever having an opportunity for redemption or atonement. This is why reincarnation is in such conflict with the teachings of the Catholic Church, which wants you to believe that salvation and redemption can only be accomplished through its intervention. The truth is that reincarnation provides the opportunity to continue on your journey to become at one with God, climbing the stairs of the pyramid on the way to the top, atoning for your actions that hurt others, and receiving forgiveness.

Revelation

I remember as the year 2000 was approaching, so many of the preachers on television were claiming that the world was heading toward a major calamity, as described in Revelation. Over and over again they cited passages out of this section of the New Testament as evidence of the pain and suffering we'd soon be exposed to. I remember one evening just before the New Year, I was scanning the channels on TV and found a religious show in which a preacher was sitting with his wife and another couple onstage. He stated that he wanted to be taken in the first wave so he wouldn't have to watch the suffering and misery that would follow. The other three individuals seated with him began to shout "Amen!" and stated they also wanted to die in the first wave.

The camera then panned to the audience, and my heart went out to these people. They were clapping in response to the declarations of the people onstage, but you could see the intense fear and pain in their eyes—and I am sure in their hearts as well.

Even to this day when I occasionally attend a Catholic Mass with my wife, I hear the sermons refer to Revelation, and it is also found in the writings of the Christian church. Revelation is the last book of the New Testament, which is apocalyptic in nature. The Christian religion often claims it was written by the Apostle John, which isn't realistic, for he would have then been more than 100 years old, if he had indeed still been alive at the time. Like the concept of the devil and hell, Revelation is used by Christian leaders to keep people rooted in fear.

The person who wrote Revelation toward the end of the 1st century A.D. was a man imprisoned on a rocky Greek island known as Patmos, a Roman penal colony. He was talking about the events occurring in his lifetime, not in the 21st century:

— In the Prologue in **Chapter 1,** he writes: ". . . for the [appointed] time is near." Nineteen hundred years later is not considered near.

He further states that "every eye will see him, even those who pierced him," referring to the Roman soldiers who "pierced" Jeshua on the cross. Are *they* still alive today?

He goes into great detail about the seven churches that were founded by Paul in seven communities—Ephesus, Smyrna, Pergamum, Philadelphia, Laodicea, Sardis, and Thyatira—stating that they would flourish again. He also writes several paragraphs in which he addresses each one of these communities. Do the majority of them even exist today?

— In **Chapter 7,** he refers to 144,000 people who will have special marks on their foreheads to show they were the "chosen" leaders of the world that would exist after the chaos and tragic events to come. The 144,000 would be made up of 12,000 Jews from each of the 12 tribes of Israel.

Not only do the Jewish people of today not know which tribes they came from, but it's hard to believe that church leaders would be willing to accept that the world would be ruled by 144,000 Jews. Do the leaders in the Vatican *really* believe and accept this? If not, then why continue to preach to people and frighten them by citing Revelation, rather than telling them the truth?

— But finally, let us go to **Chapter 18.** The writer of Revelation states that the merchants are going to cry because they won't be able to bring their cargo—which includes gold, silver, myrrh, frankincense, chariots, and slaves—to the markets of Rome, for the city will have been destroyed. Are we still delivering chariots and slaves to Rome?

There is so much more information in Revelation that can't be interpreted in any way other than to suggest that the author was talking about events he was predicting would happen in *his* lifetime.

He concludes by advising not to "seal up the prophetic words of this book, for the time is near," reiterating the warning in Chapter 1. What does "near" mean? Does it mean 1,900 years after he wrote these words, or during his lifetime? Obviously these events *didn't* happen in his lifetime . . . nor will they ever happen.

Satan

As I previously mentioned, if you are going to have a hell, naturally you must have some entity that calls it home. Well, say hello to Mr. Devil.

The concept of Satan actually originated in the 6th century B.C., at that time referring to one of God's angels. But eventually the word *Satan* was used to describe someone in a negative light, similar to our calling terrorists Satan or Saddam Hussein referring to America as the great Satan. It developed into an expression meaning a bad person or someone we should dislike, but not a supernatural evil force. In the Hebrew Bible, as well as in Judaism to this day, Satan never appears as he does in today's Christianity, as the leader of an evil empire. He first appears in the Hebrew Bible, the Old Testament, where he is portrayed as not necessarily evil, or even opposed to God.

In the Old Testament, Satan often appears as an angel who, rather than being an enemy, *assists* God. In the book of Job, the angel Satan has a conversation with God, where he suggests that Job be given a series of trying circumstances in order to judge his loyalty to God.

In Numbers 22:23–33, Balaam is on his way to collaborate with enemies of the Jews, and God sends his angel Satan to stand in the way of the donkey Balaam is riding, in order to prevent him from continuing on that path. So Satan is depicted as an angel God would use for certain tasks, not as an evil entity.

But things change dramatically in the New Testament. Christian leaders changed the concept of Satan to cast this "fallen" angel as God's rival. So he became an enemy and counterpart of God, an antagonist to God. This portrayal of Satan definitely caused some problems in the religion's efforts to control the people.

Some of the Roman intellectuals rejected Christianity. They asked: *If the Christians claim that their God controls the universe and everything operates under God's will, then how could there be the possibility of evil spirits or supernatural forces in the universe? Shouldn't they be subject to the will of God, Who rules over all?*

But the church's response was that these opponents were being influenced by Satan and demons, which explained their false declarations. In the efforts of early Christian leaders to create fear and to further control the lives of the populace, the concept of the devil was important. Just as the church was the only conduit to God, so could it alone protect the people from being influenced by the devil. This aided Christianity's cause tremendously in subsequent years, enabling it to torture and murder many thousands of people who it could claim were under the spell of the devil. Even almost 1,300 years later, witch trials were held in Salem, Massachusetts, where innocent women and men were hanged by officials who claimed that these people's souls had been taken over by Satan.

Isn't it now time for Christian leaders to tell their followers the truth—that there *is no such place as hell* or an evil entity known as the devil? Isn't it now time to tell them that these concepts were established 1,600 years ago to incite fear in the hearts of the people in order to control their lives, and this practice should not still continue today?

Jeshua's Death and "Your Sins"

Perhaps the most difficult of all things to talk about is the death of Paul's friend, his Savior, his brother, and a man he loved beyond words. I can't begin to express to you what being in his presence was like. In his presence, one felt peace, joy, serenity, hope, and a closeness to God that is indescribable.

Jeshua's love for people was extraordinary. It wasn't of the type one might have toward the person one chooses to marry, but rather was like the love a parent has for a child, or like that between a brother and sister who really care for one another. His love for people was real, never pretended. The same was true of the compassion he had for others, regardless of who they were. He didn't distinguish between the poor and the wealthy, those with power and those who led simple lives. To him, they were all God's children, all were his brothers and sisters, and his love for them was truly blind.

Jeshua's death on the cross has already been described to you. Christian leaders took it upon themselves to shift the blame for his death from the Romans, and instead declare that the people of the world were responsible. They manipulated the truth by claiming he died for the sins of those living today—*your sins*—as well as those who lived in the past.

During the approximately 300 years of the Inquisition, hundreds of thousands of innocent people were brutally tortured and murdered by religious officials, their crime being that they didn't accept the doctrines of the Catholic Church. In the Silesian town of Neisse, a huge oven was constructed, and over a ten-year period, more than a thousand children, some as young as two years old, were roasted alive to punish their parents. I cannot accept that Jeshua's life was given up so that those who committed these crimes that are beyond comprehension could be forgiven.

During the Holocaust in the 1940s, Germany was a country in which 95 percent of its citizens were Christian. Nazi representatives took the lives of millions of innocent people, including young children, who were thrown into crematoriums. Were their heinous crimes forgiven on a daily basis, a weekly basis, or at the end of the war when the American and Russian armies liberated the concentration camps? I cannot accept the idea that Jeshua died so that *their* sins would be forgiven.

In recent years we've learned how the lives of children in countries throughout the world have been destroyed by pedophilic priests. Did Jeshua die on the cross so that these priests could be forgiven as they committed these crimes 2,000 years later?

And last, do leaders of the Catholic Church believe that Jeshua's loved ones stood around the cross as he was dying and counted how fortunate they were, for now their sins were being atoned for? And when children are taught today that Jeshua died on the cross because of them—so *their* sins would be forgiven—what transgressions do Church leaders claim the children have committed that would justify the death of our beloved Savior?

Do they have any idea of the impact that they, the Church leaders, are having on the lives of those children, who are trying to process and reconcile the guilt they feel, thinking that they are responsible for Jeshua's death? Don't they understand that children then torture themselves trying to imagine what possible sins they could have committed to have caused Jeshua to die?

Throughout the ages, millions of people have been damaged by the guilt the Church has laid upon them. The Church has basically made an industry out of the death of our beloved brother! It wasn't his death that he would have wanted us to celebrate, but *his life;* messages; and teachings about universal love, compassion, and living in truth.

It is with a heavy heart that I write these words. I will cry with you and Catholic leaders as we envision Jeshua's death together. I will laugh as we remember his incredible sense of humor, and I will dance and sing as we remember his tremendous passion for life. I will be humbled alongside you and these leaders as we recall his enormous acts of love and compassion for all. But I will not celebrate his death with the Church leaders, nor will I transfer the blame for it onto the lives, hearts, and minds of the 1.2 billion people who have attempted to live by the doctrines of a church that has tried for 1,600 years to enshroud its followers in fear and guilt.

Forgiveness is an enormous gift. And we offer it to Catholic leaders, upon whom hundreds of millions depend for their relationship with God and Jeshua . . . followers who believe they can only have such a relationship through the Church.

Yes, Church leaders are offered forgiveness, but it comes with a price: we need their acknowledgment of all that has been done that is wrong, which would be unacceptable in the eyes of God and Jeshua. And from this acknowledgement needs to come genuine, heartfelt remorse. Then indeed, forgiveness can be theirs.

A New Beginning

There are so many wrongs that have been perpetrated over the last 1,600 years, including the invention of a hell and a devil to inspire fear in the hearts of those who look to Christianity for guidance; and the creation of the concept of original sin, again so that followers live in fear of the wrath of God.

And most of all, the religion's need to have us believe that *we* are responsible for the death of our beloved Jeshua, for we are all "sinners." It must stop!

Do the current Catholic leaders have the courage to acknowledge the truth? Do they have the courage to open the gates to their secret archives and let the world read the scriptures as they were originally written, which will confirm the truths I have disclosed in this book? Do they have the courage to acknowledge to the world that the Jewish people were not responsible for the death of Jeshua, and that the Church has used them as scapegoats for 1,600 years, encouraging suffering beyond words and imagination?

In the next chapter, we shall explore the role of women in the Church today. It, too, is a discouraging story, yet one that must be addressed.

Chapter 20

WOMEN AND THE CHURCH

Perhaps this would be a good time to ask ourselves a key question: *what is the purpose of religion?* Let's try to understand why religion is important to humanity.

All those who accept that there is a Supreme Being want to have an understanding of their relationship with that Higher Power, Whom we'll call God. The role religion should play is to assist people in knowing how they may communicate with God, and what God expects of them as far as their values and behavior are concerned.

At different points in history, humankind's image of God has changed dramatically. One has only to look to the Old Testament to find, at various times, an angry God, a warrior God (wanting His people to go into battle and kill their enemies), and a benevolent God.

But all of these interpretations have been human made. This is as true of other religions as it is of the Catholic faith. Clearly, the other Christian denominations have been greatly influenced by the information the Catholic Church has disseminated as it relates to God and the foundational beliefs of Christianity.

Take, for example, the representation of God presented to us by the Church. We are told that the Pope speaks for God, and that the doctrines of the Vatican have been Divinely mandated. Let's examine how this has affected women's ability to participate in the activities of the Church.

First of all, in the eyes of the Catholic Church, God is a man Who is only referred to as "Father," never "Mother," and always with the masculine pronouns *He* and *His*. We're given an image in the Old Testament of a robed man with long hair, a beard, and sandaled feet, sitting on a throne.

But what if God didn't have long hair? What if God had a crew cut? And instead of a beard, what if the Almighty was clean shaven? What if God was wearing a pair of jeans and Nike sneakers? And rather than being an elderly man, what if He was a very young one?

On the other hand, what if God did indeed have long hair? And perhaps wore mascara and lipstick . . . because the Supreme Being was a woman? Why isn't that just as feasible?

I don't know what God looks like, and I don't believe there is any mortal in the world who can honestly claim to. But I'm sure, in my heart, that God is not exclusively represented by a male personage, and that it was never the intention of the Divine for women to be discriminated against.

My heart breaks when I think of how women have been treated by the Christian religion. I have already shared with you how this came about—how 1,600 years ago, when the New Testament was rewritten, church leaders intentionally altered complimentary remarks that Paul made in his letters regarding his women apostles; how they changed their names to those of men; and how it was falsely claimed that Paul decided that only men should hold positions of authority in the church, when in reality he had just as many female administrators.

Paul appointed women to the same positions of responsibility in the church as men held. The church leaders had no right to change the words in the scripture and, in Paul's name, put women in an inferior position and deny them the credit they deserved for the role they played in helping these new Christians understand their relationship with God and Jeshua. Of course, today's church leaders aren't responsible for the actions of those who lived 2,000 years ago. But it is they, the church leaders of today, who have a responsibility to rectify this situation. The time has come to allow women the right to serve God and Jeshua, and enjoy a status equal to that of men.

Abuse of Nuns

Within the Catholic Church, today only men are allowed to be priests. Women have the option of becoming nuns and are considered subordinate to the members of the male clergy. Unfortunately, it has also been confirmed that thousands of nuns worldwide have been unable to keep their vows because they have been raped or coerced into having sex by priests.

The Vatican recently made the extraordinary admission that it is aware, after years of receiving complaints, that priests from at least 23 countries have been sexually abusing women. Confidential Vatican reports obtained by the *National Catholic Reporter,* a biweekly magazine in the U.S., have revealed that members of the Catholic clergy have been exploiting their spiritual authority by requiring sexual favors from nuns, including demanding sex in exchange for such things as certification to work in a certain diocese.

The Vatican acknowledges that there are countless cases of nuns having been forced to have sex with priests. Some were required to use birth control; others became pregnant and were encouraged to have abortions. In one case, 29 sisters from the same congregation became pregnant by priests in that diocese. The Vatican has tried to downplay the gravity of this situation, hiding behind a veil of silence, and only recently issued a statement: "Certain negative situations must not overshadow the often heroic faith of the overwhelming majority of religious nuns and priests."

I've been told by colleagues of mine in Europe that some of the historic monasteries and convents scattered throughout Europe are close together, separated by fields. When these fields have been excavated for development, it has been discovered that they contained unmarked graves of babies who had apparently been born out of wedlock, the result of intercourse (or rape) on the part of priests and nuns.

Pedophilic Priests

Most people had no knowledge of the scandalous behavior of some Catholic priests until recently. But now, of course, their pedophilic activities have become well publicized throughout the international media. But these aren't events that have just become commonplace in the last 50 years. The sexual abuse of young children by the clergy has been going on for hundreds of years, originally being reported in the Middle Ages. It most likely began at the time women were excluded from the priesthood, which means it has probably been occurring since the Church was formed. Can we even imagine the pain and suffering that these children experienced?

But none of this has to continue. The time is *now* to allow women to hold the priesthood. The time is *now* to allow both male and female priests to marry and have families.

Would this create a less qualified priesthood? No, just the opposite. There are many wonderful, committed priests today within the Church. But to allow women to become priests and permit them all to marry and have families would surely put an end to the sexual abuse perpetrated upon the nuns, as described above, and it would also eliminate pedophilic behavior, for men with those predilections would no longer find a safe haven within the priesthood.

Catholic leaders distorted the position of Paul with the claim that he didn't allow his priests to marry. How has this practice benefited the Church? It brought about a disgraced priesthood that for hundreds of years has attracted men who were pedophiles. This has caused great injury to other devoted priests who were not, as well as to the reputation of the Church itself. Similarly, the Church has been deprived of devoted women, dedicated to Jeshua, who were—and are—denied the right to enter the priesthood.

The changes I'm recommending would have an immediate impact on the world, if only Church leaders have the courage to implement them. Let us hope and pray that they will see the light, and let's do everything we can to give them the support they will need.

Seth Speaks

We're now coming to the end of this journey we've been on. In the next chapter we'll review the challenging issues I've discussed in this book, along with solutions and ways we can work together to effect change. But first I want to talk about my personal link to this material.

Even if Paul and I don't share the same body, we share the same spirit, soul, and beliefs . . . and the same commitment: that it's time for a new beginning—a time for truth.

I live with a duality, and I don't distinguish Paul's thoughts or feelings from my own. I express myself through my conscious mind. Paul expresses himself through my soul mind. But we are connected and inseparable, as *you* are with your own higher self.

In the early 1960s, a woman by the name of Jane Roberts began to verbally channel messages while in a trance. The channeled voice identified himself as an extremely advanced spirit, using the name Seth. The messages that Seth relayed through Jane Roberts became published in books collectively called *The Seth Material.*

It was recently brought to my attention that in one of Seth's channelings more than 40 years ago, he stated that the spirit of Paul would reincarnate at this time, and that in the 21st century, Paul's reincarnation would correct the mistakes the Church had made. Seth claimed that a period of spiritual awareness would then be ushered in. I am committed to accomplishing what Paul believed he had begun 2,000 years ago.

Chapter 21

Time for Change

It's been several days since I wrote the previous chapter. I knew that I needed some space before I could write this last one. Something kept telling me that Spirit had a message for me before I could start. Last night I sat at my desk and invited Spirit in. I let my mind go to a state of quiet and stillness, making an effort to set aside my conscious mind, and waited for a message to come.

This is what Spirit asked of me:

> *Yes, Nick, there is tremendous support for you from those who love you in the spiritual dimension. We want you to succeed in touching the lives of people all over the world. You must remember: the intent is to show them the truth and bring them the light so they may improve their lives, so they can make great strides in becoming at one with that part of God that is inside of them.*
>
> *As for the Catholic Church, do not meet this challenge in anger, but rather in love, with a gentle passion. It is your responsibility to show it the way, to be a beacon of light to lead it out of the darkness.*

Let it be done with respect and compassion. That is your challenge. To bring change through logic, love, and truth . . . so that even those who are at fault will feel comfortable in joining you.

The following appeal is not only being written to *you,* but also to everyone else reading this book along with you who is interested in the truth and a new beginning. It's also being written to the priests and nuns around the world who take their instruction from the Vatican, as well as those in the clergy who are in intermediary positions between these local representatives and Rome. And most important, it is being written to the hundreds of administrators in the Vatican, those who truly control and manage Catholic policies and doctrines.

I will be using the pronoun *we* as I address the Church administrators, for these words represent the sentiments of God, Oneness, Jeshua, my angels and guides, and hopefully *you* and others all over the world who are reading *Time for Truth* and share our sincere and heartfelt concern that there is a need for change. . . .

And we say to you who are in the Vatican, surely you must be aware that in the country of Italy, where your headquarters are located, Catholics represent 97 percent of the entire population. Yet only 30 percent of these people attend church. Certainly you must be asking yourself why this is so.

And we ask why in France, where 76 percent of the people are Catholic, only 12 percent attend church.

And we ask why in Ireland, where 90 percent of the population is Catholic, only 50 percent attend church.

And we ask why in Germany, where more than 30 percent of the population is Catholic, only 13 percent attend church.

And we ask why in the United States it is estimated that only around 32 percent of Catholics attend church.

The percentages are consistently low for countries all over the world. Surely you must be aware of these statistics. Have you not asked yourselves why so many of the 1.2 billion Catholics in the world are turning their backs on the Church? Where is the Church failing them?

These messages that we bring to you—the leaders in the Vatican, as well as the leaders of all the Christian religions in the world—are important. And we say to you that it is time for you to open up your hearts, minds, and souls and accept the truth. It is time for you to have the courage and the integrity to acknowledge all the wrongs committed in the name of God since the inception of the Christian religion. It is time to truly ask for forgiveness for all the heartache and pain that people have suffered over the last 1,600 years as a result of some of the actions of the religion's leaders. You are not responsible for the decisions these leaders made 1,600 years ago, but you are responsible for the continuation of those decisions.

It is time to tell the people the truth: that there is no such place as hell . . . that it was named after the dump outside of Jerusalem that burned 24 hours a day 2,000 years ago . . . that the concept of hell was created by Christian leaders to put fear in the hearts of their followers.

It is time to tell the truth: that these leaders invented the devil to instill fear in people in order to control their lives. Sixteen hundred years ago they distorted the teachings of Jeshua and turned words of love into words of fear, and this should end now. It is time for you to declare that you will no longer use the power of fear, but instead embrace and teach the power of love. If you also accept the love of God and Jeshua inside of you, you will recognize that it is time for a new beginning.

And we ask you, plead with you, to no longer place the burden of guilt on God's children, claiming that they are all sinners. Do away with the ludicrous and childish story of a serpent in a garden persuading a woman to convince her husband to take a bite of an apple that God forbids him to. And banish the belief that because of this, God has punished every person who is born; that only you can save them; and that if they do not submit to the required ceremony and join your religion, God will condemn them and send them to your fictitious hell. Can you not see how damaging this doctrine of original sin is?

Can you not see, you who are the leaders, how mature, intelligent, and caring people of the Christian faith are turning away from you for insisting on the existence of a punitive God and teaching that every person in the world who does not accept these childish and hurtful teachings are going to be punished and will go to hell when they die?

It is time to acknowledge that this was a fairy tale made up by Augustine in the 4th century and ask forgiveness from those innocent souls who have been tortured and killed over the last 1,600 years for not accepting these beliefs. It is time for a new beginning.

And we ask you: how much longer are you going to blame the death of Jeshua on the Jewish people when you know that it was the Romans who crucified our beloved Christ? It is time to acknowledge that there was never a trial held by the Jewish elders that condemned Jeshua, but rather, this was a fabrication by the Romans and Christian leaders, for they did not want to take responsibility for his death; and that for 1,600 years of history, the religion has encouraged, or been directly responsible for, the torture and murder of millions of people of the Jewish faith in order to perpetuate its false allegations and discrimination against these people.

It is not just a matter of your discontinuing these false teachings and telling the truth, but you in the Vatican must ask from the very depths of your hearts and souls for forgiveness for the pain and suffering the Catholic Church has caused. And we say to Pope Benedict XVI: you recently brought back the Latin Mass, again making these false accusations against the Jewish people in your Easter services—a Mass that Pope John Paul II intentionally discontinued, for he knew it was wrong. We say to you in the Vatican, it is time for a new beginning.

As for Jeshua dying on the cross and your claim that he did so because of the sins of your followers, this is a very sensitive subject. We do understand that you are trying to honor Jeshua by claiming he loved the people so much that he was willing to die for them. But why do you have to associate that love with guilt? Do you really believe this is right? Why must you try to create a society of people who believe that they are responsible for his death and should be filled with guilt over it?

Has it ever occurred to you that accusations of that nature may be one of the major reasons why people are uncomfortable going to church? It is ironic that on the one hand, you have been blaming the Jews for his death; and on the other, you have been blaming 1.2 billion Catholics, claiming that he died because they are all sinners and he wanted their sins to be forgiven. There is no logic to this, but regardless, it is time for a new beginning. If you need guidance in determining how to deal with this issue, we who are in Spirit are prepared to help you.

As for reincarnation, this may be difficult for you to accept, after hundreds of years of denying its existence. It is not necessary for you to try to grasp something that may be so foreign to you—even though it was the belief of Jeshua and most of the leaders of the Christian religion for the first several hundred years following his death, and even though it states several times in the New Testament that John the Baptist was the reincarnation of the prophet Elias. But you have left the world with a 6th-century resolution, adopted by the fifth ecumenical Council of Constantinople, declaring that anyone who continued to believe in reincarnation would be excommunicated and cursed.

It is time for a new beginning. Withdraw your resolution, and have the wisdom to recognize that there are hundreds of millions of your brothers and sisters on this planet who do believe in reincarnation. If you cannot understand reincarnation or accept it, so be it, but do not condemn others who do not share your beliefs. It is time for a new beginning.

Can you not recognize the tremendous benefit to you and your 1.2 billion followers if you allowed women equality within the Catholic Church and the right to hold positions in the priesthood? Can you not recognize the tremendous benefit of allowing priests, both men and women, to be married and have families of their own? Can you not envision the extraordinary number of dedicated men and women who would be inspired to enter the priesthood if they were also permitted to have spouses and children? There is absolutely no justification for not proceeding immediately with these changes. It is inhumane to do otherwise. It is time for truth, and it is time for a new beginning.

There is a desperate need right now for some organization to step forward and lead the people in bringing peace and harmony to our planet. The world needs an organization that can inspire and motivate people to embrace universal love and compassion and to live in truth.

Now is the time for your Church to become that leader. Your Church, unlike a government, is international. It has a presence around the entire globe. Christianity represents one-third of the world population, including the 1.2 billion Catholics. Your Church can become the creator of the "new beginning" and make The Great Tomorrow a reality.

To accomplish this, you must first acknowledge the truths as discussed in Time for Truth *. . . and can you envision what the worldwide response would be to Christianity if you were to accept the changes that we who are in Spirit are asking you to make? Perhaps you are concerned that the followers of Christianity would be angry with you if you were to admit the truth and incorporate these changes. But that is not what would happen. If you had the courage to make them, your followers would embrace you with love and respect. You would no longer have half-empty churches during your services around the world. Instead, they would not be large enough to accommodate the hundreds of millions who would attend services who presently are not doing so.*

Yes, it does take courage, but we and many others will help you make this transition. And yes, there will be some at the Vatican who will reject these changes and will want to continue with the old practices—practices that are false and have resulted in the Catholic Church failing in its mission. Then let them have their own following and their own assignment of churches, for they will soon find themselves extinct.

Change your teachings to recognize that we are all brothers and sisters, that we are all children of God, and that God loves all of his children, no matter what religion they choose to practice. Let us together create a new world—a world with peace and harmony among all people, who, led by your Church, totally embrace universal love and compassion and live in truth.

We promise you, if you sincerely ask for forgiveness for the mistruths, hurt, and heartache that people have been living with since the 4th century, you will be forgiven. You have been told that there is no greater sin than to commit one in the name of God. These changes <u>must</u> be made in order for Christianity to survive. Together, we can create a new beginning, a Great Tomorrow.

In previous chapters I shared with you that I asked Spirit if it was their intent for *Time for Truth* to destroy Christianity, and they answered me, "Not destroy, but to *save* Christianity." And we truly, truly hope the church leaders will join with us in saving Christianity. It can be done.

A Request for Your Support

Isn't it now time for all people of the world to love one another as brothers and sisters? Isn't it time to agree that no longer will those of other religions be threatened with punishment by God and damnation to hell if they don't accept Christianity's teachings? Let's join together, and may our churches and temples stand side by side. From each of our steeples let there be an invisible silver cord that rises to the heavens and entwines with all the cords from all the steeples from all the churches, connecting them to God, in a spiritual relationship beyond words.

Will you join me in also being a messenger for God and Jeshua? There are many ways in which you can help and participate. You can form local groups in your community, and together, meet with the priests and clergy in your own area. Encourage them to contact their superiors—whether they be bishops, archbishops, or cardinals—so that you can also meet with higher church officials. Motivate them, encourage them, inspire them. Do everything within your power to give them the courage to in turn contact the administrators at the Vatican. Inspire them to spread that same energy, that same rationale of common sense and truth, so that they, too, can become messengers for a cause that our society—*our world*—desperately needs.

My test-reader support team (whom I discuss in the Acknowledgments) and I have created a Website where we can meet as often as you like: **www.NickBunick.com**. Here, we can discuss efforts that are working, and deal with resistance we need to overcome. We can exchange new ideas on how to accomplish our goals. We will help each other ascend the stairs of the pyramid, to become closer to being at one with God and Christ Consciousness.

There are so many things we can do together, but most important, we can change the world we live in . . . if we are successful in getting the church leaders to accept what we're proposing. And we *will* be successful, for we have God, Oneness, Jeshua, and our angels and guides on our team.

It can't be done without your help. It is time for a new beginning. It is time for the Great Tomorrow. Let's make it happen together.

God bless you as you continue on your journey.

Afterword

Well, here we are at what *appears* to be the end of our journey together . . . but it isn't really. Instead of this Afterword being the beginning of the end, I would pray that it is the end of just the beginning. I would rather believe that we have many things we can do together in the future.

But first let's discuss what we have experienced up to this point. . . .

I made a challenge to you at the beginning of *Time for Truth*. I said that if you were a believer in God, your relationship with Him would be enhanced during your journey with me. And I stated that if you were an agnostic or atheist, you would hopefully have come to accept that you are indeed a child of a Divine Source, Whom we refer to as God.

I've shared with you some of the "444" experiences that I and others close to me have had. I'm positive that many of *you* have had such experiences while reading *Time for Truth*. I know that to be a fact, for even my test readers told me that they began to have them.

As you are aware by now, a 444 experience is your spirit guides' way of letting you know that they are with you, and is a symbol of the power of God's love for you. If these 444 experiences aren't evidence of Divine intervention, does anybody have an explanation that could account for this phenomenon? I hope you'll join us at our Website, read some of the 444 experiences others have had, and share your own.

Along our journey, I've shared with you many of my channeled messages. Some were given to me from Spirit for you, others were personal to me, and some were for all of us. I've always found these channeled writings fascinating, for not only do they contain profound information and advice, but I'm also acutely aware of the fact that they are coming from a spiritual dimension, from entities far more evolved than I am. And oftentimes the writing styles have been very different, even the poetry.

And I shared with you profound Divine messages Rasha received from Oneness and Christ Consciousness. If these writings aren't coming from sources within the spiritual realm, then what other explanation is there? Neither Rasha nor I possess the skills to have written those words.

As I've been sitting here in front of my computer, I've occasionally been looking out the window to see the very location where thousands of white dovelike birds sat on the lake on those two remarkable days I described in Chapter 5. I'll never forget the way those birds responded in unison to almost every move I was making, and hearing the whooshing of angels' wings twice above my head. There is no explanation other than Divine intervention.

And then I introduced you to Sara, the miraculous gift God gave her, and her personal story of being healed in an instant from incurable cancer. God performs miracles through her every month—hundreds every year. I talked to Sara on the phone recently. She sends you her love.

I shared a story of how Spirit saved my life on an icy road, as well as the experiences I've had with some of the most gifted psychics on this earth—Duane Berry, Laurie McQuary, and Janet—who all told me I had walked with the Master 2,000 years ago and would be communicating with you in the future . . . which is now, *today.* And regarding reincarnation, I shared with you my dream of my last lifetime in France, which was confirmed in so many ways.

There are so many other places we have been together on our journey, including the cleansing of our souls through forgiveness. You may have made this journey of spiritual healing in two days, or it might have taken several months. But either way, that's fine. The important thing is that we took it together.

Then we came to the part of our journey involving events of 2,000 years ago, where I hope you gained a greater understanding of what really took place before the messages of Jeshua and Paul were distorted by early Christian leaders. And we examined the consequences of those distortions and how they have affected the world—in the past, as well as today.

During the months I've been writing *Time for Truth,* many of the concerns about the Catholic Church I've shared in this book have become front-page headlines across the globe. In almost every country in Europe, outrage is now being expressed toward the Vatican for the behavior of pedophilic priests who have represented the Church for many, many years—as men and women who were abused as children have stepped forward. There is also strong evidence that the Church has been hiding this information from the public and the authorities. It has come to light that the action Church officials took was to transfer the priests responsible for the abuse to other dioceses, where they just continued their perverted and criminal behavior.

I'm committed to doing everything possible to try to persuade those individuals in the Vatican who manage Church policies and doctrines to accept my suggestions, as found in this book.

As I wrote at the beginning of this Afterword, it's my hope that this is not the end of our journey together, but rather, the beginning. I'm asking you to join me—and help me—so it is *our* mission, not just mine. Together we can make this a better world, one embracing universal love and compassion, and where we are living in *truth.*

Together we can create *a new beginning* and a Great Tomorrow.

— **Nick Bunick**

Acknowledgments

After I had written the first two chapters of this book, I realized that I wanted to be able to evaluate what I was composing, but I was too emotionally and spiritually involved to be able to do so. Was I making my point? Would my readers be able to understand what I was trying to convey? I really didn't know if I was always able to be objective. So I made a decision that I would select six individuals who could help me by being my test readers. I didn't know if this was normally done by authors, but I really felt that I needed other people to read the material as it was being created and get their reactions.

So I proceeded to contact six people, four of whom had never met each other previously, from three different parts of the world. One was from Europe, two from different parts of Canada, and three from the U.S. Half were men, and half were women. They came from totally different backgrounds, and they only had two things in common: all six of them believed in reincarnation; and all six were on a spiritual path in their lives, although at different levels, which would be expected of any six people.

As I wrote each chapter, I would e-mail it to them for their comments. We shared a common e-mail address so they could discuss their thoughts among each other or with me, with every person having the benefit of reading the others' remarks. At times they didn't agree with each other or agreed on some point that *I* didn't agree with *them* on, and at times we explored ideas together. It was not unusual for someone to suggest that I articulate something a little more clearly or expand on a comment I wrote that they thought needed further explanation.

Their input was tremendously valuable; and I'm very grateful for their support, inspiration, and critiques. At one point when they hadn't received anything from me for two days, they even admonished me: "Get to work, Nick. Where's our next chapter?" I loved their energy and their enthusiasm.

I would like to introduce you to my six test readers:

— **Wilja Witcombe** was born and raised in Germany, has spent considerable time in Sri Lanka, and is currently living in India. Wilja is an extremely bright individual, with a no-nonsense type of personality. Her purpose in life is empowering people and guiding them to practical spirituality, which she describes as an approach to living that helps humankind close the gap between rich and poor nations and mitigate religious hatred, as well as promoting individual awareness.

Wilja's father was Catholic and married her mother in a Protestant church, which resulted in his getting excommunicated from the Catholic Church. This caused him great pain during his life, and today Wilja does not practice any religion but is, however, deeply embedded in her spiritual beliefs. I am tremendously grateful for her suggestions, insights, and support these past several months. (Wilja and my next test reader have co-founded a Peace Project, which involves proving the validity of reincarnation, which they believe will in turn promote peace in the world.)

— Say hello to my next reader. He lives in central Canada and is an intellectual with a heart of gold. He is a peacemaker, always encouraging me to be gentle and kind in my writing. He is committed to working for peace, with a focus on the Middle East, which he is deeply connected to.

At times when things became very tense, I could always count on his sense of humor and wit to bring calmness to the discussion. Like Wilja, he is spiritual, yet committed to the roots of his faith. He is currently developing a Website that will be linked to ours, so you may get to know him better. He prefers to remain anonymous at this time.

— My next test reader is one who wrote me a letter about 11 years ago after reading *The Messengers,* a letter that was long and rambling; and I thought, who is this crazy guy? Over the years I've come to respect and develop a warm place in my heart for **Murray Ayers,** whom we know as Mur. Mur lives in eastern Canada and became very involved years ago in the 444 Website that was created.

I have watched Mur evolve over the years into a very sensitive person who is also a channeler of messages from the spirit world. He has his own Website, **http://agentlewhisper.info**, where people from all over the world participate in discussions on different spiritual subjects. I'm very grateful for the support and help he has given to our group.

(I was informed today that last Thursday, February 11, 2010, Mur passed away. He was very committed to this book and its purpose. Mur, we love you, and you will always be in our hearts and minds.)

— I'll introduce my next two test readers together, for both ladies live in my home city, and the three of us would meet once a week in the same local restaurant and discuss what they had read in my most recent chapters. Their names are **Beth Livingston** and **Debbie Naone**, and they are on a spiritual path, upon which they've both made great strides. Both come from traditional Christian backgrounds, so their reactions to what I was writing were very important to me.

It was always a joy to meet with them weekly and answer their questions and get their feedback. They have developed their own company called Purposeology: **www.purposeology.com**. Purposeology is a coaching practice dedicated to the advancement of human consciousness through individual coaching, workshops, and retreats. Beth and Debbie often kept me inspired, and I'm very appreciative that their energy and input was available to me.

— My last test reader and I have spent many hours over the last couple of years e-mailing each other regarding the spiritual philosophies we have in common. **Bill Hawkins** is from Memphis, Tennessee, and has been intensely pursuing his spiritual growth. He asks hard questions and will not accept soft answers.

Bill is the kind of guy who will fight with you when he thinks you're wrong, and will fight *for* you when he knows you're right. He's a great guy to have in your corner, and I'm very grateful for his strength and spiritual support. Bill was always there for me whenever I needed him, no matter the reason. Thank you for your dedicated commitment.

So, to my six test readers, know that I love you and cannot tell you how grateful I am for your continued support and for encouraging me to be stronger when I needed to be, and more gentle when I was too strong. You are the best!

It is now time for me to acknowledge the tremendous support I've received from the staff at Hay House, the publisher of this book:

To Reid Tracy, the president and CEO of Hay House, I'll never forget the phone call I received from you after you read my letter telling you that Spirit had awoken me two nights in a row at 4:44 A.M., instructing me to contact you. I wrote you that I had a book inside of me that your company must publish. Without your courage to call me, as well as your enthusiasm when you told me to "go for it," none of this would have happened.

And to Jill Kramer, the editorial director at Hay House, who first read my letter and then passed it on to Reid. You've been magnificent in selecting the members of your staff to work with me, and in leading our team across the goal line to accomplish our purpose and our mission. (Please forgive the analogy. I wrote this on Super Bowl Sunday!)

And last, to Alex Freemon, the editor Jill assigned to me. Alex, you have been brilliant in providing me your comments, your evaluations, and your suggestions. Every time I thought I had it perfect and thought my work was done, you showed me time and again how to improve upon it—where to clarify things and expand on my ideas and thoughts.

I had written every chapter as if it were a book in itself. The energy and guidance from Spirit was so great that I only concentrated on each chapter being written, without thinking of the chapter I wrote before it or what was to come after it. But through your professionalism and patience, Alex, you taught me how to reorganize the chapters, combine some, and put them into a logical sequence for our readers.

Thank you, Hay House. You are the best.

About the Author

Nick Bunick was a successful businessman who fought his way up from the poor streets of Boston to living the American Dream. Then incredible spiritual events occurred in his life that convinced him and hundreds of thousands of others that he had lived 2,000 years ago as the Apostle Paul. His story became a bestseller in 1997 *(The Messengers),* and has dramatically changed the lives of thousands of people. Since then he has witnessed incredible miracles. Through years of personal research, communication with some of the most spiritually advanced people on our planet, and information provided to him from the spiritual realm, Nick is on a unique mission to share the extraordinary truth of what really happened 2,000 years ago with the world.

Website: **www.NickBunick.com**

CONTACT THE AUTHOR

When *The Messengers* came out in 1997, we provided an address for people to write to us, and we also listed phone numbers. This created a problem, for we received more than 10,000 letters in the first six months, and it was impossible to respond to everybody. Of those we did respond to, many began to write to us on a regular basis, which created an even greater logjam. My staff and I felt bad that we couldn't answer all of the mail. The same is true of the phone calls—we had four lines that were constantly jammed.

For those reasons, we've decided that instead of a mailing address and phone numbers, we would provide a Website in order for you to reach us:

www.NickBunick.com

There will be a place for the media to click for TV and radio interview requests, talk-show invitations, and magazine and newspaper features. We will make every effort to reply to inquiries within 24 hours.

We'll also keep you posted as to when I will be doing speaking engagements, and when Sara O'Meara and I will be doing symposiums in the U.S. and other parts of the world.

We'll provide places for you to click to share "444" experiences, your evaluation of the sacred-bird incidents, and any other subjects you wish to discuss. We'll also help you form action groups in your area based on the creation of *A New Beginning* and *The Great Tomorrow,* and to persuade the Church to adopt the suggestions found in this book.

We're committed to making our world a better place to live, and to doing everything in our power to help foster universal compassion and love around the world. We welcome your ideas and involvement. It will take many dedicated people, but I know we can do it. As I have written, an idea of God's cannot be defeated; and we have God, Oneness, Jeshua, and our angels and spirit guides on our team.

There are many changes that must be brought about, but with your help, I know we can be successful.

Love and blessings to each of you.

— **Nick Bunick**

NOTES

NOTES

NOTES

NOTES

NOTES

NOTES

Hay House Titles of Related Interest

YOU CAN HEAL YOUR LIFE, the movie,
starring Louise L. Hay & Friends
(available as a 1-DVD program and an expanded 2-DVD set)
Watch the trailer at: **www.LouiseHayMovie.com**

THE SHIFT, the movie,
starring Dr. Wayne W. Dyer
(available as a 1-DVD program and an expanded 2-DVD set)
Watch the trailer at: **www.DyerMovie.com**

ANGEL NUMBERS 101, by Doreen Virtue

THE OMG CHRONICLES: One Man's Quest to Discover What God Means to People All Over the World, by Peter Rodger
(available March 2011)

PAST LIVES, PRESENT MIRACLES, by Denise Linn

THE PRIEST AND THE MEDIUM: The Amazing True Story of Psychic Medium B. Anne Gehman and Her Husband, Former Jesuit Priest Wayne Knoll, Ph.D., by Suzanne Giesemann

3 CDs by Brian L. Weiss, M.D.:

REGRESSION TO TIMES AND PLACES;
SPIRITUAL PROGRESS THROUGH REGRESSION; and
REGRESSION THROUGH THE MIRRORS OF TIME

REPETITION: Past Lives, Life, and Rebirth, by Doris E. Cohen, Ph.D.

TEMPLES ON THE OTHER SIDE: How Wisdom from Beyond the Veil Can Help You Right Now, by Sylvia Browne

VISIONS, TRIPS, AND CROWDED ROOMS: Who and What You See Before You Die, by David Kessler

WRITING IN THE SAND: Jesus and the Soul of the Gospels, by Thomas Moore

We hope you enjoyed this Hay House book.
If you'd like to receive our online catalog featuring
additional information on Hay House books and products,
or if you'd like to find out more about the
Hay Foundation, please contact:

HAY HOUSE

Hay House, Inc., P.O. Box 5100, Carlsbad, CA 92018-5100
(760) 431-7695 or (800) 654-5126
(760) 431-6948 (fax) or (800) 650-5115 (fax)
www.hayhouse.com® • www.hayfoundation.org

Published and distributed in Australia by:
Hay House Australia Pty. Ltd., 18/36 Ralph St., Alexandria NSW 2015
Phone: 612-9669-4299 • *Fax:* 612-9669-4144 • www.hayhouse.com.au

Published and distributed in the United Kingdom by:
Hay House UK, Ltd., 292B Kensal Rd., London W10 5BE • *Phone:* 44-20-8962-1230 • *Fax:* 44-20-8962-1239 • www.hayhouse.co.uk

Published and distributed in the Republic of South Africa by:
Hay House SA (Pty), Ltd., P.O. Box 990, Witkoppen 2068 • *Phone/Fax:* 27-11-467-8904 • info@hayhouse.co.za • www.hayhouse.co.za

Published in India by: Hay House Publishers India,
Muskaan Complex, Plot No. 3, B-2, Vasant Kunj, New Delhi 110 070
Phone: 91-11-4176-1620 • *Fax:* 91-11-4176-1630 • www.hayhouse.co.in

Distributed in Canada by:
Raincoast, 9050 Shaughnessy St., Vancouver, B.C. V6P 6E5
Phone: (604) 323-7100 • *Fax:* (604) 323-2600 • www.raincoast.com